HOMEROOM 109

"I have been blessed and honored by a former student of mine, Chad Koons, who is featured in Chapters 5 and 6. Chad was so excited about the publication of this book that he asked me if he could design the cover for it, and he did a wonderful job! Thank you, Chad, for all you hard work. Chad is now Pastor Chad Koons, is married and has two beautiful children, and is currently serving as an associate pastor at his church."

DR. SANDRA JENKINS COOK

ISBN 979-8-88751-231-0 (paperback)
ISBN 979-8-88751-232-7 (digital)

Christian Faith Publishing
832 Park Avenue
Meadville, PA 16335
www.christianfaithpublishing.com

Printed in the United States of America

Written as encouragement to those serving God by living His truth and carrying His light into public school classrooms.

Contents

Introduction

When I was very young and heard the call from God to become a missionary, I did not know what a missionary was or what a missionary really does. My family did not attend church, so I had very little knowledge about Christianity. I, therefore, concluded mainly from movies on television that, as a missionary, I would probably be going to a foreign nation someday and would be living in poverty, helping other people who lived in poverty.

I grew up, got married, bought a home, and started working. But deep within my heart, I knew that there was still that call on my life, but I did not know how to pursue it. Asking God to lead me to do what He wanted me to do with my life, the strong desire to become a teacher enveloped me. Enrolling in a community college, I began the pursuit to obtain my degree to teach in high school public education.

Upon graduating ten years later from Shippensburg State University, I started my teaching career, unexpectedly, as an instructor at the community college. God was preparing me for the future. Obeying the continuous callings and direction from God, I developed a business program and taught at a Christian high school, became a teacher at an area vocational high school, and ultimately obtained further educational degrees to accept administrative positions at various public vocational high schools.

As I pursued the educational and professional path that the Lord laid out before me, it became clear that I was being sent by God as a *missionary* to high school students. The Lord revealed to me that missionaries are simply His disciples that obediently follow His calling to go wherever He sends them and participate in the movement of God's love to the people they are sent to. We are actually all to be missionaries wherever God places us or sends us.

Having served more than twenty years in high school vocational education in public schools, I continue to carry a personal burden for the students and staff of these educational systems. I have experienced the blessings and horrors of teaching in public education. I have also experienced the anguish of being an administrator.

On May 7, 2015, on the *National Day of Prayer*, I was asked to lead the *Prayer for the Educational Mountain* at the Capitol Building in Harrisburg, Pennsylvania. I developed my thoughts, integrated them with some researched thoughts of others, and prepared and delivered the following prayer, which was, and continues to be, an urgent prayer for our public schools:

> Dear Heavenly Father,
>
> We are here today because we need to repent as a nation and seek your face. We, your people, are in a fight for the destiny of our country right now—a destiny that will ultimately be determined by our children and by how their minds are molded and how their hearts are prepared.
>
> Father, you have blessed our nation and lifted up our nation as an example of what a nation can do when founded on Your Word— You have continued to bless us as we function in Your wisdom.
>
> You established our nation as a nation that was destined to arise in wisdom, a great wisdom that would be released to the world.
>
> You bathed our nation in creativity and innovation. You blessed us as our nation developed a culture that embraced faith in You, as laws were developed in obedience to Your commandments.
>
> In the past, this culture of Christian faith was established and was passed onto each gener-

ation, and was endorsed and nourished through our educational system.

Father, our society has failed You. Many in our country no longer esteem their Christian heritage, and, therefore, have concluded that these foundational principles and experiences that formed our society are no longer valid.

We have left our next generation without any sense of definition or direction resulting in the uprising of a generation that does what it pleases as it appears right in their own eyes.

We repent, Father, as we confess that our country has turned, and has placed our children on the altar of secular humanistic education and entertainment.

We come before You today, dear God, to ask Your Spirit to rise up within our educational system, and cleanse it.

We pray that You would raise up Godly leaders at our schools. Lord, direct them in their decision-making that they make righteous ·decisions based on Your Word, not political correctness. Raise them up as faith models to their staffs and students. Give them courage and strength as they lead.

Lord, we pray for our teachers and instructors. Touch their hearts and minds, Lord, to present Your truth. Give them a true and committed love for their students. Anoint them with the gift of teaching.

God, we pray for those that prepare and approve the curriculum materials that are presented to our children. Father, raise up a new group that will honor Your Word and promote Godly choices.

Father, we pray for the safety of our children on all campuses throughout our nation. We ask for protection from the enemy that roams our schools seeking to steal our children, kill our children, and destroy our children.

Lord, bring peace to our schools. Bring Godly unity and love to our campuses.

God, we pray that there will be personal miraculous encounters with Jesus by our children in our schools. We pray that our children will have visions and dreams of Jesus and that they will personally and individually see His Word made manifest.

We pray that blueprints and revelations from Heaven will be given to the children and that they will begin to speak out all that they see.

We pray that a great breakthrough will be released into the United States in the areas of creativity and innovation that will come through our students that will significantly impact the economy of our society.

Lord, we pray that Jesus will bring healing to our children's hearts and bodies and minds.

We pray that our children will meet Jesus and will receive the Gospel truth, and that they will then boldly tell their friends and their families about the Jesus they meet.

God, we ask that You release Your Holy Spirit upon our schools, their leaders, their teachers, their staff members, their students—our children.

God, be glorified, once again, in this great country that You have established. May our children rise up each day within our schools and proclaim *one nation under God.*

Father, we bring our worship and praise before You. We offer up these prayers.

In the mighty and holy name of Jesus we pray.

Throughout the chapters of this book, I will share my missionary experiences, highlighting the miracles that the Lord did, centering in on my calling at one particular public vocational high school. God miraculously sent His light into that school and I know that He placed me there *for such a time as this.*

I believe that the Lord will continue to send His light into the darkness of our public schools through those called to this mission field who obediently go forth in His love to serve.

To God be the glory for all He has done and all He will do!

1

You Need to Know Where I'm Coming From

For I know the *plans I have* for *you,* p*lans* to prosper
and not to harm, *plans* for hope and a future.
—Jeremiah 29:11

Not everyone who has a skill or great knowledge in a particular subject or trade area can become an effective teacher. I believe that teaching is a gift and a calling that goes beyond presenting and explaining a subject or demonstrating a skill. I believe that teaching is an anointed communications talent given by God—it is a gift. This gift, when bathed in Godly love and respect, and used in living testimony to spread the Gospel message, becomes a ministry.

So how did I become a teacher, assigned to Homeroom 109? In order for you to fully appreciate the miracles of *Homeroom 109,* I need to explain to you where I come from and how God prepared me for this calling.

What would you do as a parent if your nineteen-year-old son who had just been drafted into the United States Army and was scheduled to go overseas told you that he was coming home on a two-week leave and was going to get married to his seventeen-year-old girlfriend, a girl who he had been dating for less than a year who was still in her senior year of high school? This was the challenge presented to my husband's parents over fifty years ago. My husband's parents considered themselves to be well-respected pillars in their church. They were both Sunday school teachers for years and participated in every project in their church. My husband's father was a long-term board member.

My family members were non-Christian, never churchgoers, who were all dealing with multiple worldly issues. My mother, at that time, was having an affair with another married man. Under the guise of taking me out to learn to drive when I was sixteen, she would ultimately use me to take her to a local shopping center parking lot where she would regularly meet her *boyfriend*. This placed me in the middle of a horrible betrayal affair that I did not want to be in. I was filled with guilt because I felt like I was participating in her unfaithfulness to my father.

My future in-laws were aware of my dilemma as I often spoke to them about it, seeking counsel and comfort. Even though they appeared interested in my problems at the time, sharing these problems with them created more alienation toward me later on as a daughter-in-law choice.

My dad, who also had infidelity issues, could not handle discovering that my mom was doing the same things he had been doing. The discovery of her affair triggered a severe mental breakdown in my father, and he eventually became institutionalized for several months.

My older brother, who was verbally and physically abusive to me, drank a lot and was suspected of being on drugs. During this time, he got married to one of his girlfriends that he had pregnant (there was at least one other girlfriend pregnant at that time).

How embarrassing and demeaning this was to my husband's parents to have their son marry into such a family. They believed that they had been the model Christian parents, and they desired a much better wife selection for their son. Unfortunately, they determined their disapproval of me based on my family and who they were, not choosing to recognize or accept who I was.

In spite of my domestic environment, I was an ongoing honor student in high school at the top of my class. I was known as a *good girl* with a good reputation by fellow students.

From the time that I was old enough, I would try to find a way to go to church, any church, with whoever would take me! I even walked to a church about a mile from my home, attending all by myself. I went forward in one of the evangelistic services at that church and was saved when I was twelve years old.

I knew at that time that I had some kind of call on my life from the Lord. As Bible reading was still allowed and promoted in public schools, I often volunteered to read—and teach—the Bible during my seventh-grade homeroom period. Unfortunately, this was the last year that Bible reading and prayer would be allowed in public schools. I did not have much Christian teaching then, but I knew that God had His hand on my life, and I knew that I wanted to share God with others.

When I met my husband, Randy, I had been praying as a young teenager to someday have a Christian husband where I would be the mom of a family that would go to church together and serve the Lord together. I believed that Randy was the answer to my prayers because, first of all, he was not only strong, smart, funny, and good-looking, but also because his family went to church. I began attending church with him and his parents when we started dating. Having dinner together at his home following church was, to me, the epitome of family togetherness. However, my husband's parents did not feel I was the answer to their prayers for a wife for their son.

You probably wonder why Randy and I decided to get married while I was still in high school and why we did not want to wait until after I graduated. It may sound crazy, but it was both a love decision and a financial decision. Really, it was. Randy was being sent to Germany for the next eighteen months. It was October, and I would graduate in another seven months. We knew that we would not have enough money to pay for his way home to get married in June after I graduated and then be able to pay both of our ways back to Germany where he would be stationed. We did not want to be apart for another whole year after I graduated. So we concluded that if we got married that October on his leave, the United States Army would begin sending me money as his wife and would also pay my way to Germany to go to be with him when I graduated. The current

Vietnam War also held an impending threat that Randy could be sent there at any time and maybe not return home. We wanted to be together as much as we could.

Official parental permission was needed for me to get married because I was under eighteen years of age. My mother was more than anxious to sign those permission papers. She reasoned that if I were married, she had completed her motherly obligation to me. This would free her and justify her plan to walk out on me and my father several weeks following the wedding.

After our wedding on October 28, 1967, the next eighteen months of my life were beyond awful. Nine days after our marriage, Randy went overseas to Germany, and I did not see him again for eighteen months. Email was not an option at that time, so our only regular communication was through letters—*snail mail.*

My mother, as she planned, moved out of our house and moved in with her boyfriend, leaving me alone with my father. When my dad became emotionally and physically dangerous to himself and to me, he was institutionalized. It became impossible for me to stay at my house with my father. Eventually, I had no choice but to move in with Randy's parents so that I could complete my senior year of high school. I lived with them, in a very tense environment, until after I graduated.

After I graduated, things did not work out for me to go to Germany. However, I was able to get a secretarial job with the state government, move into an efficiency apartment downtown near the government offices, and save enough money over the next year to put the down payment on a house when Randy came home.

I often wondered and asked God why I had to go through so much emotional pain as a teenager. It wasn't until I was counseling and comforting a hurting teenage student years later that I understood. God had prepared me to be able to minister to teenagers down the line who would desperately need my help. I was able to understand their hurt, and they were able to relate to me because I had been there and had experienced similar things that they were facing.

After Randy came home from Germany, was discharged, and we were settled into our new house, doctors informed us that I was physically unable to have children. In the face of that disappointment, the Lord put a calling in my heart to become a teacher. Although I already had a full-time job, I entered college as a full-time student. I took this step of faith even though I was newly married and had the bills of purchasing a house and the expenses of starting out in life. Within a year and a half, I completed my first two years of college at Harrisburg Area Community College. I then transferred to Shippensburg University to begin working toward a Bachelor of Education in Business.

During my first year of attendance at Shippensburg University, the Lord performed a miracle, and I became pregnant with our first son. I immediately postponed my college career and began raising a family as a stay-at-home mom. The Lord continued to bless our family, miraculously giving us a total of three beautiful children: two sons and a daughter.

When our oldest son entered a Christian school in Harrisburg in his first-grade year, the Lord spoke to my heart once again and said that I was to return to Shippensburg University and, upon graduation, develop a high school business program for the Christian school that my son was attending. The program was to encompass grades 9 through 12. I was to create, implement, and teach the business curriculum at the school. However, at that time the Christian school only offered classes from kindergarten to the eighth grade.

After our daughter, our youngest child, began kindergarten, I received a very strong nudging from the Lord to return to Shippensburg University and complete my educational degree. Upon graduation, I sent a letter of application to the Christian school, expecting to immediately embark upon the calling of beginning the business program. Much to my surprise, I was told that the school was not looking at expanding and was not interested in developing a business program at that time.

In light of what I viewed as a setback, I hesitantly accepted a summer offer from Harrisburg Area Community College to become the Instructor of Secretarial Science. Shortly after accepting the position, the other instructor working in my department tragically became ill with cancer and was hospitalized. The college was unable to find another quick replacement, so I was asked to continue the teaching responsibilities for my assigned classes as well as cover all the classes that had been assigned to the other instructor.

I soon discovered that the Lord was using the summer position, with all the added responsibilities, to prepare me for the task of developing the business program at the Christian school. The additional courses that I had to cover required me to become thoroughly skilled in all the vast variety of business courses that I was to create and teach. The Lord prepared me in the essentials of business education so I would fully comprehend what levels of skills would be required of high school business students preparing to enter a post-secondary school. More simply stated, I was being trained to prepare the curriculum for the Christian high school business program that I had been called to establish. God knows the plans he has for us and prepares us for every task He calls us to perform.

One week before area public schools were to start up that fall, I pulled into a Sears parking lot to purchase school clothes for my children. The Board President of the Christian school pulled in next to me. He jumped out of his car and came over to me in the parking lot and excitedly asked, "Are you still interested in that position at our Christian school, and can you begin by teaching typing?"

The Christian school board had decided to add the high school business program that God prepared me to create. Even though I had just been offered a full-time instructor position at a terrific salary at the area community college, without a blink, I answered, "Yes!"

He then stated that the school could not financially compensate me and, furthermore, lacked the necessary equipment for the program, such as typewriters. I responded that the Lord never promised that I would be paid. He had called me to create and teach a business program and graduate a class of students from the Christian school. Because it was His plan to be performed in His timing, I knew the Lord would provide everything that I would need to be able to accomplish the calling He had given me.

A week later, I resigned from my position at the community college to begin my volunteer position as the typing teacher and physical education teacher (yes, they needed me for that position as well) at the Christian school.

During the next five years, the high school business curriculum was developed together with college prep curriculum to expand the Christian school's grade offerings from K–8 to K–12. Through God's faithfulness, each year the Christian school was able to add an additional grade level until they were able to graduate their first class, consisting of three graduates, two college prep and one business prep. That was thirty years ago, and the Christian school has remained a K–12 school to this day.

Then our oldest son decided he wanted to go to a public junior high school to play football, and I was faced with a tough decision. I knew if he were to leave the Christian school, his brother and sister and I would also have to leave because the rule at that time was that all your children had to attend the Christian school in order for you to teach at the school. If I did not continue teaching at the school, we would not be able to afford having our other two children attend, as the school had given us free tuition in place of giving me a salary.

After much prayer, I received peace about allowing our son to transfer schools and for me to leave my teaching position with the Christian school. Therefore, we all left the Christian school, wondering where the Lord would lead us to next, believing that He still had plans for all of us.

2

Missing the Mission Field

*I give thanks to Christ Jesus our Lord, who has given
me strength for my work. I thank him for considering
me worthy and appointing me to serve him.*
                                    —1 Timothy 1:12

After leaving the teaching position at the Christian school, even though I believed I had made the right decision, I immediately felt there was a void in my life. I missed serving the Lord in active ministry every day. I longed to be working on the *educational mission field* again, and I prayed fervently that God would place me back in His service somewhere, somehow.

With a desire to stay in the teaching field, I signed up with our area's public school district to be placed on their list as a substitute teacher. God already knew where His plans would lead me.

Amazingly, I was called two weeks before the beginning of the school year to go in for an interview at the area vocational high school. They needed someone immediately to fill the position of a long-term one-year substitute to be teaching keyboarding and recordkeeping.

When I received the telephone call inviting me for the interview, which came directly from the Principal of the high school, I was in the middle of painting our upstairs bedroom. I told him I would be interested in interviewing for the position and asked when it could be scheduled. He replied that he wanted me to come in right away—that afternoon. He said that he had reviewed my application and was impressed with it. I explained that I was painting a room, and I was a mess. He urged me to immediately get ready and come in, promising that the job would most likely be mine if I did. Therefore, I quickly shut down my painting project, got cleaned up and dressed, and within an hour, was at the school for the interview.

The interview with the Principal turned into more of an introduction to other administrators and staff and a tour of the school rather than an interview. The Administrative Director and the Administrative Assistant Director of the school joined the tour, which culminated at *Homeroom 109*, the classroom to which I would be assigned.

I was immediately offered the position as a long-term one-year substitute, which I accepted, and was welcomed as their new hire. This is the way God seems to work in my life. He plans it. He does it. It happens!

That first day of school for me was definitely enlightening. I discovered that the former instructor of the classes that I would be teaching had taken sabbatical leave to acquire her Librarian certification. She had such a bad experience in the classroom while teaching the students that I would be teaching that she vowed she would never come back to the school as a classroom teacher—only as the Librarian.

As the bell rang for students to go to homeroom, I could hear students coming my way. It was not what I expected. They were cursing loudly and proclaiming nasty things they wanted to do to the teacher of the class, assuming the former teacher was in the classroom. Boy, did I begin to pray hard. God is faithful. Miraculously, He gave me favor right away with the students. His presence was evident and took over. He filled me with a beautiful love and respect for the students, which I know they immediately felt. I recognized that these students were different from the students at the Christian school, yet very much the same. They were teenagers in search of their identity and worth. I knew that God had placed me in another mission field, one that became much more challenging.

Following homeroom, I began receiving classes. I was scheduled to teach seven forty-five-minute class periods, each with different groups of students assigned by vocational programs. I would have a forty-five-minute lunch period and one class period free for planning. The regular school day, therefore, would be comprised of eight full class periods.

The organization of the classroom was set up for disaster. There were thirty student desks and chairs in the classroom, three side-by-side double rows of ten desks. For each of the double rows, the five right-hand desks were equipped with IBM Selectric typewriters, manual typewriters from the 1960s that had a spinning ball printing element that could easily be removed, was somewhat fragile and not designed to resist frequent handling—not a good selection for classroom use. The five left-hand desks remained clear to accommodate a student textbook with room to do written work in recordkeeping. I hope you are getting the picture of a chaotic classroom environment of thirty students, three double rows of students sitting side by side, half of them doing typing on loud manual typewriters as they are seated beside the other half working on textbook recordkeeping assignments. The reasoning for the arrangement was based on the limited availability of only fifteen typewriters. With such a setup, I was doomed to be a referee, not an instructor. I immediately began planning rearrangement remedies.

The eighth-period class, the last class of that first day, was the most interesting. The Auto Mechanics and Auto Body students were scheduled to come to my class. To my surprise, three administrators, including the Principal, the Assistant Principal, and the Assistant Director, arrived unexpectedly before the class arrived and stood in the back of the classroom. I figured they were there to observe how my day was going. Instead, I later found out that they were there because they were worried that they would be needed to protect me from this particular group of students!

As the automotive students approached my classroom, I could hear them making loud, vulgar, and threatening remarks aimed at the former teacher. They really sounded angry. Upon entering the classroom, they were stunned and somewhat disappointed that I was there instead of the former teacher. They apparently wanted to release their steam. They wanted to know who I was and where the other teacher was.

Surprisingly, they did not appear to be surprised or intimidated by the administrators being in the room. I found out later that there were regularly one or more administrators in this particular class with the former teacher to control them and assist the teacher.

Once again, I experienced the awesome presence of the Lord as He gave me confidence and control of the classroom. I know that He supplied me with the humorous, witty comments and responses that I was able to make that not only calmed the students down, but also won them over. He enabled me to radiate His love, a true love and respect for the students that they could feel and trust. The administrators, appearing quite amazed and pleased, left the classroom after being there for only about ten minutes.

After school was over that day, the Principal came to my room and explained how awful that same class reacted last year to the former teacher. It was to the point that an administrator had been assigned to that class period everyday. The students were not only threatening the teacher, they were threatening her family as well. This was the reason that the former teacher left and the reason why the administration was so desperate to fill the position.

In spite of the poor choice of equipment and curriculum that I had been required to use for the course, I managed to revamp the course and successfully complete my year as the long-term substitute. I had really grown to love the students, and I believed that most of them liked me.

The former teacher was scheduled to return from her sabbatical to reassume her position. However, she had completed her new certification that year and was reassigned as the Librarian. The keyboarding and recordkeeping teaching position was now formally available, and I was asked to accept the full-time position as the instructor, with the offer to count and bridge my substitute year as a tenure year.

I really wanted the position but said I would only accept the position if the administration would agree to change the curriculum for the course. I felt that the students deserved a better course that would support their career goals. I suggested that a computer lab be installed offering the students the opportunity for Keyboarding and Computer Applications training.

After some debate, the administrative team accepted my suggestion, and the Board approved and installed a computer lab in the classroom. I was hired to create the new curriculum and teach Keyboarding and Computer Applications as a full-time instructor, residing in *Homeroom 109*.

What I thought would be a one-year substitute experience turned out to be a permanent teaching position and missionary assignment that continued for the next sixteen years. God answered my prayer and assigned me to another *educational mission field*.

3

Not at Public School!

If the world hates you, know that it has hated me before it hated you. If you were of the world, the world would love you as its own; but because you are not of the world, but I chose you out of the world, therefore the world hates you.

—John 15:18–19

Choose this day whom you will serve… But as for me and my house, we will serve the Lord.

—Joshua 24:15

Absolutely loving my new assignment at the vocational high school, knowing that God had placed me there, I was anxious to witness and experience everything that God was planning to do. From the first day on the job, I began answering my classroom telephone with "Things are fine in 109!"

Looking through my rose-colored glasses, as I am so often guilty of doing, I assumed that God had also spiritually prepared the school administrators and leaders to be ready and willing to welcome and support my ministry assignment. Having come from the Christian school environment, I was unfamiliar with the blatant rejection of Christianity occurring in the public school system that I would soon personally experience.

Every student at the vocational high school was assigned in their tenth-grade year to take and complete my course entitled Keyboarding and Computer Applications. If a student transferred to the school in eleventh or twelfth grade, they were assigned with the tenth grade class to take and complete the course. What an awesome blessing—and responsibility—to have the opportunity to touch the lives of every student at the school!

The vocational high school was a *comprehensive* vocational high school—meaning that both academics and vocational training were provided by the school, and students would obtain their high school diploma from the vocational high school. In many of the other area vocational high schools, only the vocational training was provided, and the sending home districts provided the Pennsylvania state-mandated academics and issued the high school diploma.

At this school, most of the students were divided into two groups, one group assigned as A-Week and the other group assigned as B-Week. Academics and vocational training alternated every other week—while students in A-Week were in academics, students in B-Week were in vocational training and vice versa. I thought this was a good plan for the vocational training as students had a full week of full days to accomplish projects. However, for academics I felt it was not a good plan. Academic teachers found that they had to spend the first part of each new week reviewing with students from their previous week-ago teachings.

There was also a smaller group of students assigned to a technical track, who were in vocational training for half the day and in academics for the other half. I personally felt this was a much better way academically for the students. The school eventually went to this type of scheduling for all students.

I taught seven out of eight class periods per day, usually having twenty-five students per class, adding up to 175 students each week or 350 total students for the two-week period. In every class period, students were all at different skill levels and working on different project assignments as they progressed through the course.

Believing that organization plays a big part in classroom management, I would strive to be completely caught up and organized for each new day in grading and documenting student assignments. Students seemed impressed, and actually secure, in knowing that I would always know exactly where each and every one of them were to be working in their assignments. I would access the computer system and mark it in my book as to where each student left off each day in keyboarding. I always had their most recent computer application project assignment graded and ready to return for them to make corrections, if needed, or to move on to the next project if approved.

One of the most important things I learned while teaching at the community college was to actually do the student assignments ahead of the students—always be one day ahead of them. Therefore, I would personally do each of the computer application project assignments ahead of the high school students so that I would know all the problems that a student might encounter on an assignment. I was exceptionally good at making *all* the errors that could possibly be made in a project. My students thought that I was really smart when I could troubleshoot their errors so quickly. It was only because I had made the exact same errors and figured out how to solve them when I did the lesson, usually the night before!

I enjoyed joining in the student typing speed competitions, and I must admit, I was proud to usually have the fastest speed and best accuracy. As the classroom was set up on a LAN (local area network) system, all the results of typing speed tests were immediately posted for everyone on the system to see. Moans and grumblings usually ensued when one of my scores was posted placing me in first place. However, I believe it did reassure their faith in me as their teacher, particularly at a vocational school, proving that I had the skill that I was requiring them to acquire. Many vocational teachers sometimes *show off* their skills to ensure their students' confidence.

Students were scheduled for my course during their vocational program week. Therefore, the grade for Keyboarding and Computer Applications was averaged in with their vocational grade. This ultimately gave me the opportunity to work closely together with all the vocational instructors.

Students were encouraged to work at their own speed and skill level to complete the course so that, upon attainment of the required skill level in keyboarding and completion of the project assignments in computer applications, they could return to their vocational program full time, often before the end of the year, if they wanted to. Some students actually wanted to continue longer in my course to expand their skills beyond the requirements. I believe that some of the students that wanted to stay had found a haven of peace and comfort in my classroom, as I know the presence of God was there for them.

God gave me a special rapport with my students. He enabled me to be on their side of the volleyball net, on their team working with them, not on the opposing side working against them. Often, I felt like the cheerleader in the classroom, encouraging each and every student, accepting their best effort and praising them for their best effort. You have to understand that many students, such as the automotive students, came to my class not thrilled that they were required to learn to type. Learning the skills on the computer did make it more palatable.

Every marking period, teachers at our school were given the opportunity to send progress reports, positive and negative, to the parents of their students. I always tried to send out encouraging reports for many of my students. I especially sent reports for those struggling students who I felt were giving their best effort, those that I knew were accustomed to receiving only negative progress reports. One young man came to me so excited and surprised to have received a good progress report and told me that his grandma had given him money because of it! I also remember another young man who asked me not to send another good progress report because his mother slapped him when she received the progress report before reading it, assuming it to be another bad report.

Many of my students began to call me *Mom*. I believe they felt like I really cared about them like a mother would. I did not hesitate to congratulate them on good choices and reprimand them on poor choices.

Instead of mingling in the cafeteria in the early morning, as most students did, there was usually a group of students, especially Monday mornings, waiting for me to unlock the door to *Homeroom 109* when I arrived. They would stand in line at my desk waiting to tell me their stories from their weekend and to share with me important events happening in their lives. These students craved recognition and advice. I fervently prayed for a stronger way to be able to minister spiritually and openly to these students.

Several weeks into my first year of my full-time hire at the school, I received a form in my mailbox requiring all teachers to sign up to advise a club. Clubs would meet on Tuesday afternoons. Instead of a regular eight-period day on Tuesdays, there would be nine periods with the last period of that day to be scheduled as Club period. Clubs would not be counted academically—they were to be an educational enhancement and were referred to as *ungraded curriculum.*

I was so excited. I believed this was my opportunity to start a Christian club at the school! I immediately completed the form and returned it to the Administrative Director's office.

The next day, I received an unfriendly visit from the Administrative Director. He was extremely angry with me. He informed me very sternly that there would be *no Christian* club at the school. He told me straight up that *no* public schools have Christian clubs and *no* public schools promote Christian views. He especially pointed out that it was not acceptable for me to promote Christian views at a public school. He tore up my submitted form, threw it in my wastebasket, and handed me another blank form to complete.

Not knowing anything about my rights at a public school or students' rights at that time, I accepted the scolding and redid the club form. Wanting to create a club that would encourage students and staff at the school, I decided to create a *Booster Club.*

It did not take very long until a large number of students signed up for the club. Our club did various projects of encouragement, such as participating in serving meals at the homeless shelter, putting together packets of trade-made and/or trade-related gifts for teachers and staff, creating hallway bulletin boards featuring and promoting various vocational trade programs as well as other clubs, and sponsoring identification contests of past high school, prom, athletic, and marriage photos of instructors and staff.

For the next couple of years, the Booster Club continued to be very popular at the school. It had an encouraging effect on the school, but I longed for and prayed for a Christian club that would have a lasting effect on the lives of students and staff at the school. It was so hard for me to realize or accept that God had actually been locked out of the public schools.

The reprimand and denial for the Christian club was followed by another disappointing visit from the Administrative Director to my classroom. The teachers and staff had all been given *The United Way* pledge forms to complete. We were instructed that everyone was expected to give *their fair share.*

As a tithing and giving Christian, I was accustomed to donating and enjoyed giving. But I believed that I was not to give to any organization where the money would be used to sponsor ungodly practices, such as abortion, and some of the organizations listed with *The United Way* did sponsor ungodly practices. Therefore, wanting to support the school effort and give, I decided to give solely to one of the Christian organizations listed under *The United Way.* I wrote a check specifically to that organization and placed it in the packet and returned it to the administration.

This time, the Administrative Director came to my classroom while I had students. He entered, fuming mad, and demanded, in front of the students, that I immediately sit down at my desk and rewrite the check that I had submitted, making it out this time to *The United Way.* He said that he could not send in the check just to one organization and have it claimed as a donation to *The United Way.* He said that there was a place on the pledge form where I could indicate that I wanted it to go to the Christian organization, but I knew that it would still benefit all the other organizations. I caved under his demand, not wanting to ignite a confrontation in front of the students. I rewrote the check and hated myself afterward for doing it.

Later, a third major Christian conflict arose within my employment position, this time because of my membership in the teachers' union. One of the first orders of business after I was officially hired as a full-time instructor at the school was my completion of the paperwork requiring me to join the NEA/PSEA (National Education Association and Pennsylvania State Education Association), the teachers' union. I was not given a choice—I was told I needed to join. New to the public school system, believing that I had to join for job security and protection, I did.

Eventually, I went on to discover that the union was a politically active force that stood strongly for abortion (calling it *family planning*) and against many of the Christian beliefs and values that I held. Publications that I would receive from the organization openly criticized Christians and promoted the pro-choice agenda, even inviting members of the union to join a march on Washington, D.C.

To bring this concept up to date, I found a current online article stating that NEA is the most influential teachers' union in the United States today, and with more than three million members is also the nation's largest labor union of any kind. According to its own website, the NEA recently asserted that it vigorously opposes all attacks on the *right to choose* and stands on the fundamental right to abortion under *Roe v. Wade*.

I became very discouraged and upset with myself over being defeated in so many areas by the public school system. However, as only God can do, He ultimately turned all these defeats into victories.

The following year, I stood up to the Administrative Director and refused to participate in *The United Way*. Instead, I wrote a personal donation check and mailed it directly to a Christian organization listed with the *United Way*. I asked them to send a letter of receipt crediting my donation to the school. The donation matched the average amount the school was expecting every employee to contribute to *The United Way*.

I wanted to maintain that I was not against giving—I was just absolutely not going to sponsor something I was against. I realized that there could be negative consequences coming to me from administration, but I decided that I would rather please God than him. I left him know that because of my Christian values and beliefs I would not participate. I also left him know that I knew that he legally could not force me to donate to a charity that I did not wish to donate to, and that he should not try to embarrass me again in front of a classroom of students. After that, I was no longer questioned about the issue, although I still continued to receive an annual pledge form in my mailbox, which I would dispose of in my classroom waste basket.

My membership in the teachers' union was not so easy to resolve and dissolve. There were only a few days in June every couple of years when a member could write a letter to the local leader of the teachers' union and request to have their membership discontinued. When that time came, I wrote my letter of resignation from the union.

However, I wanted to substantiate the integrity of my reason for leaving the union. I wanted to be sure that the local union understood that I was not quitting in order to avoid paying the membership dues; I was leaving because of my personal spiritual beliefs.

Membership dues at that time were $500 per year. Therefore, I wrote three checks that I included with my letter of resignation with instructions on how they were to be dispersed.

One check was written for $200, payable directly to the local teachers' union. My donation of $200 was more than what the local union received from their share of the national and state union membership. The local school union was to use this money to assist with the cost to send flowers to local members for various reasons and to fund other local causes and initiatives that benefited the staff at the school.

A second check for $200 was written payable to the homeless shelter in the area. A third $200 check was written payable to *Teen Challenge*, the local teen drug and alcohol rehab center. These two donation checks were to be submitted to the organizations with the local union receiving credit for the donations.

Every year, for as long as I was at the school, I repeatedly made these same donations. I purposely chose to give $100 above the dues to show that I was not leaving the union to save the money. I was leaving the union based on my Christian beliefs. The leaders of the union appreciated and respected me for this, as they would always stop by *Homeroom 109* and drop off all the same printed documents that union members received at their meetings.

The *Booster Club* continued to be a very popular club at the school for the next several years. You will discover in an upcoming chapter how God moved in a miraculous way to eventually answer my prayer for a Christian club.

4

Stroke of Grace

And we know that all things work together for good to them that love God, to them who are the called according to his purpose.

—Romans 8:28

With the installation of the new computer lab in my classroom came the responsibility to administer the LAN (local area network) system. This was all new to me, so I had to go through training. I still needed to obtain twenty-four more credits to maintain my teaching certification, so I decided to enroll at Harrisburg Area Community College to obtain an Associate of Arts degree in the Computer Applications Specialist program. This would satisfy the credits requirement and provide the additional training I would need.

Oftentimes I am guilty of overloading my plate, and it was certainly more than full during this hectic time of my life. Not only did I have all the new and demanding requirements of my teaching job, including more college courses to complete, I also had my family responsibilities as a wife and mother, which were at their peak. Trying to sustain the schedules for three teenagers, ages thirteen, fourteen, and sixteen, who were involved in school plays and sports and other after-school activities, not to mention all their other *need-to-have-a-life* events, took up most of my afternoons.

Even with all the individual activities of our family, I want to emphasize that we always all sat down together at the dinner table every weekday evening for our meal and family discussions. Saturday morning breakfasts together were also standard procedure—I always cooked a special family breakfast, and we enjoyed the food and shared highlights of our week.

We all had our Saturday house-cleaning assignments. In addition to their own wash (each assigned specific days of the week for washer and dryer use), each of our children had their own bedroom and one other main room to clean on Saturday. I did the kitchen and all the bathrooms and my husband headed up any house or auto maintenance or outdoor project. Saturday evenings became individualized according to social activities chosen by each of us.

Sundays started with an *every-man-for-himself* breakfast, followed by Sunday school and church, then out to eat after church, then a nap, and often Sunday night church or other family activity.

Right in the middle of everything organized and busy that seemed to be going so well, I began to experience severe dizzy attacks. The room would begin spinning around and my blood pressure would zoom up really high.

During one of these attacks, while at home on the telephone, I felt like I was hit in the forehead with a hammer. I fell backward on the couch where I was sitting. I could not get up and could not walk for about an hour. As soon as I could get an appointment, I went to the doctor, who ordered several tests to be performed at the hospital. It was determined that I had experienced a TIA (transient ischemic attack).

My speech was slurred, I had lost my balance and had to hold on to furniture or the wall to walk, and my memory database was messed up so that I was reciting my telephone number as the one from when I was a child and calling my dog by the name of a dog I had as a child. At school, I had to hold onto the edges of the student desks in order to balance and move around the classroom. The doctor was considering placing me on disability.

During this time, the Lord began urging me to visit a little country church near our home. I had never gone to that church, but the Lord kept drawing me to visit. So one Sunday, I had to bribe my family to visit the little rural church, promising them a Sunday lunch buffet at a great nearby restaurant.

When we went to the church that Sunday, we were really surprised to discover that there were very few people in attendance, mostly country-looking, Pennsylvania Dutch, farm-type people. We wondered why the Lord would guide us there. Our home church was one of the bigger churches in the area, with people of different races and various professions, so this was definitely a culture shock. Our family filled an entire wooden pew, and we certainly stood out in that sparsely filled sanctuary.

Following the service, a gentleman who claimed to be a board member, came to greet us. He asked the normal questions of who we were and where we were from, and then amazingly added that he felt that when he saw us enter the church that morning, the Lord had shown him that we were going to become the church's Youth Leaders that they had been praying for the Lord to send.

Not long after that introduction, the Pastor approached us and asked what our ministry was, declaring that he felt that the Lord was telling him that my husband and I were to become the church's new Youth Leaders that they had been praying for the Lord to send. We were astonished at both declarations, in that there were hardly any youth in attendance that morning at the church.

I was especially confused at why the Lord would want me to be a Youth Leader when it was obvious that I would not be able to physically lead a youth group. I could barely make it down to the altar to pray! I knew my husband would help with the sound and support of the ministry, but I would have to be the one actually planning and leading the services and activities.

The Pastor asked if he could visit us at our home that week, and we agreed to meet with him and pray about the request. So we met and prayed with the Pastor, learned more about the church, and heard more about his testimony of God speaking to him about us. By the end of the evening, we decided that if the Lord wanted us to be the Youth Leaders, then we would do it. I personally believed that if He was calling me to serve in this way, He would enable me to do it. Therefore, we accepted the call to serve as the Youth Leaders, to begin as soon as their Board would be able to meet and approve us.

The next morning, when I woke up and got out of bed, I realized that my balance had been restored. I did not have to hold on to anything to walk to the bathroom. I began praising the Lord out loud and realized that my speech was no longer slurred—I was completely healed! I knew this was confirmation from God that He had called me to do the youth ministry and that His anointing would be on the ministry.

At our first youth service the following week, we had five teenagers in attendance, with two of them being our own children. However, within a month we had over thirty teenagers attending the Wednesday night youth service. We had such a large group that the Pastor gave us the sanctuary to use because we had more teenagers attending Wednesday night youth service than adults attending Wednesday night Bible study!

Within three months, we had over one hundred teens attending the service, with most being students from the vocational high school where I was teaching. All of this was in God's planning for the school ministry that was soon to explode.

5

Welcome to the Club

I will go before thee, and make the crooked
places straight: I will break in pieces the gates of
brass, and cut in sunder the bars of iron:

—Isaiah 45:2

Are you kidding me? The masonry students entered my classroom to begin keyboarding classes, and there was the student with the broken arm in a cast from his hand to his elbow. Why would a student with his hand and arm in a cast be scheduled to take keyboarding? Typing is a hands-on skill, and there was no way that this student would be able to learn to type this way. I tried to have him sent back to his vocational program, but it was his instructor's free prep period, and I was asked to keep him and find something for him to do. It made no sense to me at the time, but God always has a perfect, miraculous plan for everything. I could not foresee all the wonderful things that God would accomplish at the school, and eventually throughout the world, through this one student.

Chad was not the kind of student that welcomed the opportunity to sit quietly and do nothing for a class period. He was personable and loved to talk. Most of the time it was almost impossible to keep him quiet. He was not rude but very respectful and extremely likeable. Even though I assigned him several computer applications projects to complete one-handed to keep him quiet and busy and learning, he managed to continue to come up with ways to lure me into conversations with him during every class. Thankfully, the cast was eventually removed from his arm, and he was able to participate in and successfully complete all the regular keyboarding assignments for the course.

Through our conversations, I learned a lot about Chad and he learned a lot about me. He was especially interested and had a lot of questions about the youth group that I led at the church. He actually lived very close to the church, and apparently his family had attended some services there in the past.

Near the end of the school year, as it was becoming warm enough to open our pool, I scheduled what we called a *Gap-Rap* as an activity for our Manada Gap Church youth group. This activity was held at our home where we scheduled several *Gap-Raps* during the summer months.

For these events, I would prepare lots of picnic food and our family would set up outdoor activities and open our pool. We would have an outdoor fire where the youth could roast their own hotdogs and marshmallows on sharpened skinny birch tree branches—some of the *citified* youth had never done this.

We had several yard games as well as a volleyball net set up in the field beside the pool area. Placing microphones, speakers, and other audio sound equipment on our patio area outside the pool alongside the field we would set up for a culminating evening worship service that always included lots of worship music and special song presentations by the youth, a sermon that contained a salvation message, and an altar call. The youth would sit on folding chairs, blankets, or towels in the field during the service.

The regular Manada Gap Youth Group members were encouraged to invite friends who were not regular members to attend these activities. All teens were welcome. For this particular *Gap-Rap*, one of the regular youth attenders invited Chad and he showed up—with his electric guitar! Yes, Chad had long hair and was caught up in worldly rock music, which he proceeded to play continuously for several hours on our front porch from the moment he arrived!

I must confess that I went inside the house to prepare more food to take outside, but more purposefully and frustratingly to get alone and ask God what I could do about Chad and the ungodly music he was playing in the middle of our Godly picnic. God's answer: "Just love him." Thankfully, God did not leave me on my own for this. He immediately bathed me in the love that He expected me to share.

At the worship service that evening, Chad gave his heart and life fully to the Lord. He began attending weekly youth group services, and several weeks later received the baptism of the Holy Spirit, and his baptism was definitely with the *fire*! He announced that he felt like he could go outside and pull up trees, roots and all, right out of the ground!

The following school year when it came time for me to complete the form to advise a club, the Lord stirred my heart that it was now time to try again to start a Christian club at the school. At the same time, the Lord challenged Chad, as His chosen student, to lead the way to obtaining the Christian club.

Through information from the Penn-Del District of the Assembly of God, we were informed that a legal case had currently being fought in Williamsport, Pennsylvania, regarding starting a Christian club at a public school. The court ruled in favor of the club because it met the federal requirements of meeting either before or after school hours or during school hours during a period of *ungraded curriculum*. The school club had been started by and was being led by a student of the school, another requirement. The Christian club at the school was also required to have an adult staff member willing to serve as the advisor to the club. God had gone before us and had everything prepared.

We managed to obtain the federal legal documents that were used to win the case for the Christian club in Williamsport. We thoroughly studied all the documents and prepared copies to be presented to the administration of our school.

Because clubs at our school met weekly during an added ninth period on Tuesdays, an extra class period of *ungraded curriculum*, we met the first federal requirement. Chad took the charge to pursue the club and lead the club as a student and I agreed to serve as the advisor, meeting the other requirements. After checking with their school solicitor, who reviewed our findings, administration was told that they had no choice but to allow the club.

Creating a Christian club inside a public school in the central Pennsylvania area was unheard of at this time. We became the first public school Christian club to be established in the area. We called the club the *Youth Alive Club*, associating it with the national group of *Youth Alive Clubs* at that time.

The club soon became the largest club in the school. Initially, we began meeting in my classroom but quickly outgrew my classroom size. We were then reassigned to meet in the cafeteria and, ultimately, the auditorium.

Soon after the establishment of the *Youth Alive Club* at the vocational high school, our daughter was able to establish a Christian club in her junior high school. Next, our middle son and our niece established a *Youth Alive Club* at another public high school. Over the next few years, other youth within the Manada Gap Church Youth Group established Christian clubs at their high schools and junior high schools. Eventually all these Christian clubs formed into what became known as the *Youth Network*.

A *Youth Network* rally, the first in the area, was held in the vocational high school gymnasium. Future rallies were scheduled at an area church and later grew to such a great size that they were held at the ball park on City Island in Harrisburg.

6

Here's Your Sign!

And these signs will follow those who believe: In My name they will cast out demons; they will speak with new tongues; they will take up serpents; and if they drink anything deadly, it will by no means hurt them; they will lay hands on the sick, and they will recover."

—Mark 16:17–20

One of the things that I didn't mention yet—Chad had a major speech impediment—he stuttered. Because of his disability, he often had difficulty verbally leading the club, particularly in presenting his devotional messages.

In our talks together, Chad had shared with me that he had started stuttering as a child. He believed that because he had intensively teased an older man with a major stuttering problem who lived in his neighborhood, that he had been given the same impairment.

Because our church was small and rurally located, it could not sponsor the hosting of youth outreach events. Therefore, we took advantage of participating in the various sectional and district youth events offered by other larger Assembly of God churches in our area. This brought our youth together with many other Christian youth groups, giving them assurance that they were not alone in their walk of faith as a teen.

Our group attended a sectional youth retreat at the Penn-Del Camp in Carlisle, Pennsylvania. There were hundreds of youths in attendance from many area churches. The worship music leaders and the evangelistic speaker were amazing. At the conclusion of the evening message, an invitation was given for all to gather at the front of the auditorium for praise and prayer.

I went up front accompanying our youth group. I was standing beside Chad when I felt that I heard the Lord speak to my heart to pray for Chad and tell him that he was going to be healed of his stuttering. I confess that I was afraid to do this openly because I was scared that if it was not really from the Lord, and it was just from within me desiring that healing, that Chad's faith might be hurt by my speaking this to him. Yet I wanted to be obedient to the Lord and not miss the opportunity for Chad's healing if this was really from God.

So I decided to ask God to confirm that He had given me this direction. I asked God for a radical sign. I asked the Lord to have the Evangelist at the podium on the center of the stage come down off the stage and walk around hundreds of others and come right over to Chad and I. Then I would know that the direction was from God and then I could tell Chad that God was really going to heal him of his stuttering.

As I was praying and asking God for this confirmation, all of a sudden, without any word of explanation, the Evangelist walked to the far left of the stage and descended down the side steps of the platform. Our youth group was standing way over to the far right of the stage and back several rows from the platform. There were many rows of others behind us.

The Evangelist, without stopping to speak or to pray for anyone else, made his way to the back of the rows of teens. He then walked behind everyone clear across the back of the entire group, moving to the right side of the stage behind where we were. My heart was pounding. Then, as though he knew who we were, he made his way though the crowd and came directly up to us.

Excitedly, I then turned to Chad and told him that God had spoken to me that he was going to heal him of his stuttering. I told him and the Evangelist how I had asked God to confirm this. The Evangelist and I placed our hands on Chad, and we prayed for and claimed his healing, and Chad immediately began to speak without stuttering. What a remarkable testimony of God's power this was not only to Chad but also to our entire youth group attending that night!

The following Tuesday at our school Youth Alive Club meeting, Chad shared this testimony with the students that attended. Several students were attending as guests that day. Most of these students had known Chad and were aware of his former speech impediment. They were amazed that he was now speaking without stuttering, and they knew that it had to be a miracle from God. Chad gave an invitation for salvation, and several of the guest students responded, accepting Jesus as their Savior.

One of the students who accepted the Lord that afternoon was a girl from the Carpentry program. She was a nontraditional student enrolled in a predominately male trade. She held her own and was respected by the guys in the program, as she also held a black belt in karate. Apparently when she had first enrolled, she was challenged by a group of her classmates. She gallantly performed a *roundhouse*, physically knocking down several of her male classmates, and henceforth received no further challenges.

The sequel to this story is sad yet victorious. The following summer this girl was living in downtown Harrisburg. The place where she was staying caught on fire and she died. Her death was tragic; however, we have the assurance that she had made a public decision that afternoon during that Youth Alive Club period to accept Jesus and she had, then and there, received her gift of eternal life with Him. *O death, where is thy sting? O grave, where is thy victory?*

Together with his gift of preaching and teaching, Chad eventually was blessed with another gift—a miracle gift of singing. When Chad first began to try to sing, I encouraged him. His early attempts were not something that most other people found pleasant to listen to. In fact, one day as I was working with Chad to practice a song, the Pastor of the church came out from his office to the sanctuary to find out what the awful sound was that he was hearing.

I thought he sounded wonderful. The first song he did in front of the church was entitled "I Am Available." He sang with all his might from his heart, meaning every word as he pledged his life to service anyway the Lord wanted to use him. The song was way off key and screechy, but he faithfully sang it in its entirety. It was videoed, and I still have a copy of it. It now serves as a documentation of the miracle that God has done.

As time went on and Chad faithfully continued to pursue singing unto the Lord, his voice miraculously became better and better. Teachers at the high school began dropping into our club meetings to hear him sing. He ultimately obtained the lead in the local *Youth for Christ* Easter program. He went on to attend *Christ for the Nations* and became a lead singer in their productions. He has evangelized in other countries, preaching, teaching, and singing. He is currently serving locally as an Associate Pastor at his church and heads up their worship band.

7

See You at the Pole?

If my people, which are called by my name, shall humble
themselves, and pray, and seek my face, and turn from
their wicked ways; then will I hear from heaven, and
will forgive their sin, and will heal their land.

—2 Chronicles 7:14

Whoever acknowledges me before others, I will also
acknowledge before my Father in heaven.

—Matthew 10:32

A small group of teenagers in Burleson, Texas, gathered together for a *DiscipleNow* weekend in early 1990. It is said that on that Saturday night, the students, broken and burdened for their friends, felt compelled to pray. They decided to go to their school flagpoles and pray for their friends, schools, and leaders. This birthed a united student-led movement of prayer that has become known as *See You at the Pole.* The vision challenges students around the world to hold similar prayer meetings at their school flagpoles, meeting and praying at a designated time on a designated day.

At 7:00 a.m. on September 12, 1990, more than forty-five thousand teenagers met at school flagpoles in four different states to pray. A few months later, youth ministers from all over the country met at a national conference in Colorado, reporting that their students had heard about SYATP and were equally burdened for their schools. It soon became clear that students across the country wanted to take part in the annual event. There was no stopping them! On September 11, 1991, at 7:00 a.m., an estimated one million students gathered at school flagpoles from Boston to Los Angeles, and the movement has since expanded to an international movement of prayer among young people. Today, more than two million students from all fifty states and more than twenty other countries participate in SYATP.

Our church youth group attended youth camp over Labor Day weekend in 1991 and found out about SYATP that was scheduled for that September. They could hardly wait to get back to school to present it to other *Youth Alive Club* members. It was an exciting yet challenging prospect. It would be an opportunity to individually step out publicly in faith at the school and be an active participant in the prayer gathering, yet it would also be a challenge to publicly stand up and be recognized for the faith. As the upcoming gathering was promoted at the school, not only did students face the challenge of publicly participating, but also staff, teachers, and administrators, particularly those proclaiming the faith.

I remember the pain and anxiety on the face of the Principal when I presented my request as the advisor to the *Youth Alive Club* for permission to schedule the event. Professing, and often defending, that he was a Christian, he always struggled with his stand of faith when it challenged his administrative duties in the public school. I know he was extremely uncomfortable when put in the position of making decisions affecting the *Youth Alive Club* that confronted the public school stand against Christianity.

After the Principal confirmed through the school solicitor that the club was within their legal rights to hold the event, permission was given to schedule it with the stipulation that participation had to be outside of official school hours. Students would be required to be in their assigned homeroom promptly at the start of school at 8:00 a.m. It was also emphasized that the event was supposed to be student-led—yes, students were to be leading in prayer! To me, this was a wonderful stipulation that students were required to be the leading *pray-ers.* The members of the club that participated that morning had no problem adhering to this directive! What a great witness and powerful anointing they all projected that day! They also used their student leadership authority to *invite* the adults in attendance to pray as well.

The event started at 7:00 a.m., and teachers were not officially *on the clock* until 7:40 a.m. Those that expressed interest in attending were concerned about whether it was *legal* for them to participate and whether participation would put their jobs in jeopardy. However, one by one a half dozen plus brave teachers and staff members made their way to the flagpole that morning supporting the students! Altogether about thirty students and staff showed up and prayed!

The flagpole was located in front of the school entrance inside the turnaround circle where the student busses came in to deliver students. As each bus pulled in, loaded with students, we could not help but observe the gazes from the busses. The incoming students were unusually quiet as they would exit the bus and enter the building. Every so often, a student, who was unable to get to the event early, would exit the bus and cross over to join the prayer group—that took added courage.

Each year, more and more students and more and more staff members met at the flagpole in September to pray for the school. Each year there would be awesome testimonies emerging from the gathering.

One year I took pictures of the gathering with my camera (the kind that needed the film developed). It was a dreary overcast morning. Several weeks later, after using up all the film, I took the film cartridge to be developed. It always took several days of waiting to get the developed pictures back. Finally, they were ready, and I picked them up, scanned through them quickly, took them to school and placed them in my desk. When I had time later that week, I decided to arrange some of the pictures on the *Youth Alive Club* section of my bulletin board.

As I began reviewing the pictures more closely, I was amazed to discover that one of the photos showed the group of students and staff encircling the flag and above them the sun breaking through a cloud in the form of streaks of light in the perfect shape of a cross! Fortunately, having had the pictures developed at a nearby drug store, it could not be argued that I had *photoshopped* the image. That special picture went right up on the bulletin board! The news about the amazing photo spread quickly throughout the school and curious students and staff showed up at Homeroom 109 to see the miraculous photo! What a great testimony of the awesome presence of the Lord at that event!

In my later years at the school, two former students who had dated throughout high school and were married following graduation, and who were both saved through the *Youth Alive Club* meetings and the Church Youth Group services, decided to return and participate in the annual SYATP event at the school. They had been married for several years and wanted a child but were unable to become pregnant. That morning, we prayed for them at the pole, asking God to bless them with a child. Nine months later, they had a baby girl and attributed the blessing to the prayers that morning.

Every year since that first SYATP gathering, staff, students, parents, Pastors, and Youth Leaders continue to meet at the flagpole at the school. And every year, there are new testimonies of God's faithfulness to their obedience.

8

Take Down Your Bulletin Board!

What was meant for evil, God turned around for good.
—Genesis 50:20

The Lord your God will go before you, and fight for you.
—Deuteronomy 1:30

That afternoon, as I often did, I stayed after the school day ended, straightening up my classroom and working on planning and grading. However, on that particular day, I had so much to do that I ended up staying beyond the afternoon, working into the evening. I ultimately discovered that this was God's plan for a *divine appointment* that He had arranged, and that He had gone "ahead of me" to fight a battle that I did not realize was coming my way.

I was not aware that the school board was holding a meeting that evening at the school. And I was definitely not aware that I was one of the main topics of discussion. Apparently, a complaint had been filed that I was displaying a Christian-themed bulletin board in my classroom. The school board was being challenged to determine whether I should be required to take the bulletin board down.

That evening, as I was working at my desk, two school board members, both women, entered my classroom. They introduced themselves, and asked me why I was still in my classroom that late in the day. I explained to them that I was completing work so I would be organized for my classes the next day. I felt quite honored that they decided to visit me, or so I thought. They obviously were not expecting me to be present in my classroom, as they acted very surprised, yet pleased, that I was there.

After some more questions about the courses that I taught, they asked if they could look at the bulletin boards in my room. I was certainly impressed that they noticed my bulletin boards and were interested in them. So I proudly led them over to the displays and asked if they wanted to see any particular materials. Bulletin boards take a lot of time to develop, and I always tried to do my best to present nice displays. Still unaware of why they were really visiting, I was thinking that I was just being blessed by a nice visit and compliments about my classroom.

Then, all of sudden, I realized why they were really there, as they victoriously zoned in on what they were really looking for. They moved directly to the back corner section of the full wall-length bulletin board on the left side of my classroom to where a one panel section held the postings of the *Youth Alive Club*. Together they excitedly looked over the postings, pointing and discussing the contents. Finally, one of them turned to me and asked why I had Christian Bible verses posted on my bulletin board.

Admittedly, I was stunned. I told them that I was the advisor to the *Youth Alive Club* at the school, and that this was the section of my bulletin board that was allotted for club information and postings. And because it is a Christian-based club, there would naturally be postings of scripture.

They then began to vigorously question me regarding my personal motives, if any, for having the scripture posted where all students would be able to see it. They emphasized that I was assigned to conduct classes everyday in my classroom for students that were not part of the club. They were concerned that students in my classes who were not in the club could be offended by the information posted on that bulletin board that they would have to be exposed to while being assigned to my classroom.

Fully understanding at this point that the visit to my classroom was not just a "random" friendly visit, and being quite shocked and feeling blindsided, I tried to defensively point out that the information on all the sections of my bulletin board was able to be seen by all students, not just the club information. But the rebuttal came that the club information, because of the scripture, might be offensive to some students.

At that point, I felt the Holy Spirit take over as I recalled the verse in Mark 13:11: "But when they arrest you and hand you over, do not worry beforehand what to say. Instead, speak whatever you are given at that time, for it will not be you speaking, but the Holy Spirit."

God stepped in. I was totally unprepared for this battle, but God already knew it was coming, and He was prepared. Unknowingly, I asked the question that triggered God's solution. I asked them if they had visited other classrooms and looked at every teacher's bulletin boards, wondering if they might have anything posted that could be offensive to some students. The key to this question was *not* the offensive containment of any other bulletin board, but the fact that there were other bulletin boards.

From my question, one of the Board members began to ask questions that would turn everything around. She asked if other instructors who were club advisors also had bulletin boards. I answered that they did, but I could only personally remember visiting a few other classrooms and observing their club bulletin boards. She went on to ask if other clubs were allowed to make public announcements about events and offerings of their club and if they do make those announcements to all students and staff over the school's intercom system. I answered that they do. She asked if other clubs were able to publish and hand out information publicly to students who are not members of their particular club. I told her that they were permitted to do that and that they do it.

Examples would be when other clubs would have fundraisers or open events. Then she asked me if the *Youth Alive Club* was permitted to do these same things. I told her that our club was *not* permitted to make public announcements or hand out any printed material about our club.

Both women smiled victoriously. They then told me that they were both women of faith and that they felt that God led them to visit my classroom to see the bulletin board personally during the break in the Board meeting that evening. They did not expect me to be there, but they felt that God had me there to substantiate their concern, a concern that they were going to deliver back to the Board. We hugged and they left my room, encouraged and empowered, to go back to the Board meeting.

The concern that was delivered that evening to the Board was that the *Youth Alive Club* was being discriminated against and was being denied equal rights that other clubs at the school were given. The women presented the challenge to the Board that if the *Youth Alive Club* bulletin board was to be taken down, then all other club bulletin boards must be required to be taken down also. And whatever rights and privileges were granted and offered to other clubs, those same rights and privileges should be granted to the *Youth Alive Club* as well.

The next morning, I found out the results of the previous night's Board meeting. The Principal came right down to my classroom shortly after I arrived at school. His reaction was priceless. He began by explaining to me what was supposed to have taken place at the meeting, and stated that he did not know what happened to turn everything around. He told me that he was amazed that the Board did a complete turn-around after their break on what they were discussing at the beginning of the meeting.

The final motion and decision that was passed instructed the administration of the school to ensure that all the rights and privileges currently given to other clubs at the school be given to the *Youth Alive Club* as well. As the Principal explained the new rights extended to our club, he handed me a form on which I would now be able to submit public announcements from the club that would be presented over the intercom and included with other morning and afternoon announcements. What was meant for evil, God turned around for good!

9

─────◉─────

Valedictorian Victory

For whatever is born of God overcomes the world. And this
is the victory that has overcome the world—our faith.

—1 John 5:4

Let no one despise your youth, but be an example to the believers
in word, in conduct, in love, in spirit, in faith, in purity.

—1 Timothy 4:12

When I think about child-like faith, I think about our daughter,
Corbyn. Her actions of love and faith as a young child were amazing.

When Corbyn was in elementary school, my husband's grand-parents gave each of our children a $300 gift to use however they wished. Both of our sons spent theirs immediately on their own desires. Corbyn, however, decided to give all of her money away.

First, she gave $100 to a teacher at the Christian school because she knew that he had a very low income teaching at the school. He and his wife just had twin boys, and she wanted to help them.

She gave the next $100 to a family up the road whose father, a truck driver, had been in a major traffic accident. He had been paralyzed and was unable to work, leaving their rather large family without an income.

She gave her final $100 to the mother of a classmate, a young boy who really needed glasses. Corbyn knew that this boy's mother

41

was not able to afford to get his glasses. Together with the $100, the mother obtained some other assistance and was able to cover the examination and glasses for her son.

Also, aware that this same boy would become very emotionally upset over any kind of failure, Corbyn always tried to look out for him. When her class had an assignment to bring a bar of *Ivory* soap to school for carving an art project, she asked me to purchase an extra bar for him because she knew he would not have one and would be upset.

Even in her preschool years, she was an organizer and helper to others. She took dance lessons, and at her first recital, we chuckled as she constantly helped to position the little girl next to her and guide her through the performance.

I noticed during that dance recital that a man was videotaping Corbyn's dance group down at the stage. Following the performance, I went down to see if the man would consider making an extra copy of the video for us. To my surprise, he was an Associate Physician that I had my appointment with when I became pregnant with Corbyn. His daughter was the little girl beside her that she was guiding through the dance.

The irony behind this was that this doctor had examined me, confirmed that I was pregnant, and had offered me the option to make an appointment to have an abortion because he felt that my children were too close together. He told me that it would be very inconvenient for me to have another baby only one year after my second son was born.

Yes, I became very angry and informed him that "If God had given me another baby, he was not going to kill my baby!" His nurse, defending him, told me that he was only trying to help! At that point, I left him know that I did not want to see him as my doctor anymore. The other doctors in the practice would be the only doctors I would see from then on, and he should definitely not be the doctor to deliver my baby!

God answered this, as he was on the delivery schedule when I went into labor. However, he got stuck in traffic during the

Pennsylvania Farm Show and could not get to the hospital in time! Another doctor performed the delivery. God is so good!

So realizing who he was, I introduced myself and informed him that I was a patient that he had offered an abortion. I told him that every time he watched his video, he should realize that the beautiful little girl beside his daughter, guiding and directing her, was the little girl he wanted to murder! That did not go over well with him, as he abruptly turned and walked away from me.

When I became pregnant with Corbyn, I prayed for a Christian name for her. I did not want a common Christian choice, such as Christina, Rebecca, or Rachel, although they are beautiful names. I wanted a different name, and the name Corbyn came to me. Although I did not think it was a Christian name, I liked it and decided to use it as it was different, and it came to me while praying. After she was born, the Pastor at my husband's parents' church, educated in Hebrew, told me that *Corban* is a Hebrew word meaning *to be dedicated unto the Lord*. It is found in Mark 7:11. How appropriate!

Even though she was loving and faithful, Corbyn was also spunky and determined. Whatever she set her mind to, she usually accomplished it and did it well.

One Sunday at church, a gentleman, who was the Coach of a local midget football team, came up to us to encourage our sons to sign up with his league. Corbyn, of course, asked why she was not invited to sign up. Stuttering, he tried to explain that it was normally boys that signed up. Corbyn decided that she was going to sign up too, and she did. Our middle son joined the *pony* team and our older son joined the *midget* team. She joined the *pee-wee* team!

At the first practice, I went with Corbyn, who was the only girl on the team. My husband accompanied the boys. We were informed that we needed to purchase a uniform, a helmet, and other necessities, including a cup. I was really relieved that it was required that the players all bring their own personal cup, as I thought it was really unhealthy the way they all slurped from the squirting water device that they used. Everyone laughed when we showed up with our water cup at the next practice!

Corbyn was the fastest runner on her team. She played tight end and was *number 81*. She did not like the roughness in physically tackling her opponent around the knees. She was fast enough to catch them and grab them by the shoulders and pull them down. She became one of the best players and was featured in a newspaper article, complete with photo of her long blond curls dangling down her back from under her helmet.

When it came time for her to move up to the *pony* team, I decided that she should not compete with the boys in a contact sport at the older age level. So she decided to try out as a cheerleader and for the color guard.

Girls already on the cheerleading squad made remarks to her indicating that she may have been a player but would not be able to make the cheering squad. This only encouraged her to practice harder to make the squad, and she did. Her former status as a player did interfere with her cheering at times, as she would stop cheering and begin yelling at the players like a coach!

During her junior high school years, Corbyn was an excellent academic student. Using her organizational skills, she became involved in the school plays as their stage manager. She also started and led the first Christian club at her junior high school, right after the Christian club was started at the vocational high school where I was teaching.

Corbyn disappointed her high school counselors when they tried to convince her not to choose to attend the vocational high school but, rather, to attend the regular academic high school. They argued that she was more academically suited for a college prep track rather than vocational.

But Corbyn chose to attend the vocational high school and enrolled in the Childcare Program. She was determined that she wanted to work with children. She was also friends with many of the vocational students attending the Manada Gap Youth Group at the church and was excited about all the things the Lord was doing at the vo-tech.

Upon enrolling at the vocational high school, Corbyn shared with me that she had prayed and asked the Lord to help her to become the valedictorian of her class so that she could present the speech at graduation and give Jesus the glory in that speech. That was truly her motivation.

Corbyn and Chad worked together to lead the Christian club at the school. When Chad graduated, Corbyn took over the leadership.

Corbyn did her best and carried the highest grades in her academics and in the Childcare Program throughout her years at the vocational high school. She competed her senior year in State VICA Skills, and took first place in the Childcare Program competition. She ultimately earned and became the valedictorian of her graduating class.

She went right to work on her speech and drafted a beautiful composition. However, an unexpected battle was to emerge.

I was at home on a personal day off from school when the telephone rang. It was Corbyn calling me from the coin-operated pay telephone in the hallway of the school across from the school administrative office. She was extremely upset and crying.

She had been called into the office of the Principal. Several other teachers, senior advisors, were there as well. She had been told that she had to rewrite her speech and remove the reference to the name of *Jesus* from her speech. She could use the term *Higher Power*, but not directly the name of *Jesus*.

It was ironical that they called her in on my day off, knowing that I would not be there personally to defend her. I was livid!

I immediately called the Principal, and he told me that the school solicitor had given the order and direction for the decision on the speech. I left him know that we, as Corbyn's parents, would be fighting this decision.

Corbyn was devastated. How could she remove the name of *Jesus*, when she had promised Him that she would give Him the glory in her speech. She was told that if she did not remove the name of *Jesus*, she would not be permitted to give the speech.

We prayed. At the time, we were partners in support of *The 700 Club*, and also in support of the *ACLJ (American Center for Law and Justice)* where Jay Sekulow was Chief Counsel. I decided to call them. Speaking directly with Jay Sekulow, he told me he would take on the case at no charge to us, and he did. Attorney Sekulow, as you may know, has also represented President Trump!

I must admit, it was really tense going back to work teaching at the school under the circumstances of fighting the administration. But Jesus fought the battle for us.

Attorney Sekulow personally contacted the school solicitor, who we found out was Jewish, and presented litigation contradicting the decision regarding Corbyn's speech. And miraculously, the *ACLU (American Civil Liberties Union)* also supported us. The school solicitor rescinded his former direction to the school, and supported Corbyn's right to give her Valedictorian speech as written.

To ensure that the school complied, *The 700 Club* sent a cameraman to the graduation and videotaped the entire speech. Corbyn's story and the video was later presented on television on *The 700 Club*. This victory inspired other victories.

10

Called to Pray

> Therefore settle in your hearts not to meditate beforehand on what you will answer; for I will give you a mouth and wisdom which all your adversaries will not be able to contradict or resist.
>
> —Luke 21:14–15

> So I sought for a man among them who would make a wall, and stand in the gap before Me on behalf of the land, that I should not destroy it; but I found no one.
>
> —Ezekiel 22:30

We are all called to pray for others. God is searching for those who will stand in the gap, to intercede for others. Praying for others is not a choice; it is our privilege.

Several administrators at the school professed to be Christian, although they were usually very cautious and guarded about displaying their beliefs. Whenever an emergency situation arose, however, they would usually call upon me, in a "coded" way of speaking, to pray.

Often, my classroom phone would ring, I would answer "Things are fine in 109," and it would be the Principal. He would inform me that there was a student in the office who was experiencing a major problem and they were unable to get the student under control. He would then ask if I could come to the office and "speak as I do" with the student. He would send someone to cover my class, and I would go to the office and enter a room alone with the student, as the administrator did not want to witness what he knew I would do. I would not only talk to the student, but I would also pray with the student if they wanted prayer—which they usually did. The Lord was always faithful to show up and work His miracle.

One of our teachers, a favorite to many including students and staff, became ill and went to the hospital. Upon examination it was discovered that she needed an emergency operation because the doctors found, what they believed to be, a dangerous malignant tumor. She was rushed immediately into the operating room.

Upon hearing the report, I went to the Administrative Director of the school at his office and asked if I could hold a staff prayer meeting for the teacher and invite any teachers or other staff who would want to attend after school in my classroom.

It was close to the end of the school day and the teacher was scheduled to be in the operating room at that time. The Administrative Director informed me that I could not publicly invite others to pray because it was against school policy to hold a prayer meeting as it would still be on school time and on school property.

Following the afternoon announcements for the students, the Administrative Director of the school came on the intercom personally and announced that there was going to be a meeting for all teachers and staff in the school cafeteria immediately following student dismissal and all teachers and staff were "required" to attend.

The meeting opened with the Administrative Director explaining the severity of the surgery that the teacher was facing and explained that she was in surgery at that time. I figured that he would probably ask everyone to remember her in their "thoughts" as they left school that day. Instead, to my amazement and shock, he asked if I would come forward and lead the entire group in prayer for the teacher!

As I walked up front, I wondered how I should pray. Should I watch what I say because I was in the school in front of certain administrators, teachers, and staff who I knew resented my Christian stand? Realizing that God initiated and ordained this opportunity to pray, I abandoned all my own thoughts and turned it completely over to the Lord. I do not remember all that I said, but I know that I was led by the Holy Spirit and that the prayer was anointed with power and faith. I know that complete healing was claimed and the name of Jesus was glorified. Wow, to think that literally there was a captive audience witnessing God's power!

The next day, everyone celebrated as we learned that the teacher had come successfully out of surgery with the miraculous report that everything went well and no cancer was found, much to the amazement of the doctors. I received many personal visits, telephone calls, and messages from numerous administrators, faculty, and staff acknowledging that they believed that God did the miracle! The teacher, upon being informed of the prayer meeting held for her, also stated that she attributed her miracle to the power of prayer and intervention of the Lord. To God be the glory!

With the power of prayer fresh in the air of the school, I felt led to begin a before-school staff Bible study and prayer group. I received administrative approval for weekly use of the faculty room beside my classroom. About a half dozen faculty started to show up faithfully. We would have a devotional, a discussion if time allowed, and conclude in prayer.

One of the teachers, a man who had never indicated to me before that he was a Christian, began attending the meetings. He was excited and really eager to participate; he was normally an energetic and happy person. Sensing the urging of the Lord, I asked him to lead one of the upcoming meetings and present the devotional. He was thrilled! The week he led the meeting, he told us that his wife had placed a note in his lunch bucket that morning, encouraging him in leading the group. He presented his devotional with enthusiasm and pride, and I admit, I was proud of him and pleased that I had listened to the nudging of the Lord to ask him to do it.

Following the Bible study and prayer meeting that morning, I reported to my assigned duty to monitor the hallway outside of my classroom, as I was assigned to do every morning. On duty with me was a teacher from a classroom down the hallway, who I would normally talk to each day as we stood on morning duty.

As we were talking, the teacher who presented the morning devotional came out of the faculty room and walked between us to head down the hallway. Apparently, he had remained after the meeting to clean up his materials from his presentation. As he came out of the room and turned toward us, I gasped and put my hands over my mouth. The other teacher on duty with me asked me what was wrong. I asked him if he had seen the face of the teacher that came out of the faculty room. He said that he had. I then asked him what he saw, and he said that he just saw the teacher. He then asked me what I saw. I was actually in shock as I told him that I saw the face of the teacher as a skeleton—literally he looked like he had a skeleton head! The other teacher shook his head, said things like "You are so crazy," "You are whipped out," etc., and turned and went down the hallway to his classroom.

That afternoon, it began to snow, and it really snowed hard. We ended up having an early dismissal, followed by a hazardous drive home. It continued to snow all that night and the next day. School ended up being cancelled right up to the weekend. The snow was very deep and heavy, culminating in the gruesome weekend task of shoveling walkways and driveways just to get out and about.

Upon returning to school the following Monday, we received the devastating news. The teacher who had led the prayer and Bible-study meeting the previous week had suffered a massive heart attack and died that weekend while shoveling out his automobile.

I was broken-hearted learning of his death, yet I felt a peace as I reflected on his joy of presenting God's Word at our Bible study that past week. I must admit, I was really shaken, though, by the vision that I had received that, to me, was almost an announcement of his pending fate. But God has a reason for everything.

The teacher on duty with me in the hallway in the mornings, upon learning of the news of the death of the teacher, immediately came up to me and stated strongly and sternly, "If I ever look that way, please don't tell me!" This same teacher, an outspoken non-Christian at that time, eventually was saved, and I believe that God used the miracle vision of that morning to inspire him. Our new hallway discussions became centered on all the things he was involved in with his new church that he and his wife and family began attending.

In another instance where I was "called to pray" was when one of the administrators, the Assistant Principal at the school at that time, who could often be sarcastic and rude when it came to acknowledging the things of God, called me into his office one morning. He asked me to sit down in front of his desk, pushed his telephone over toward me, and demanded that I call God on the telephone. Confused and quite shocked, I asked him what he meant. He said that he heard that I said that I talk to God, and so he wanted me to call God on the telephone in front of him and show him how I talk to God.

Fortunately, I know the Holy Spirit took over and led me in how to answer. I pushed the phone back at him and said that I did not need a telephone to contact and talk to God. I could talk to God anywhere at anytime without a telephone. And I assured him that he could too, through prayer. In fact, I asked him if he would like to pray right there and then and he could talk to God himself. I even assured him that God would answer him. He then asked me to leave his office. He did not realize it, but this encounter triggered me to begin to pray earnestly for him for his salvation.

God answered my prayer for him using God's sense of humor. I scheduled a trip to take some of my students to downtown Harrisburg to participate in the State Civil Service Exam that was given in the spring. My husband, the night before I was to drive the students to the exam site, tried to warn me about taking the school van into the parking garage as the van might be too high to fit under the low-hanging cement ceiling beams inside the garage. I confess that I would often hear my husband's voice speaking to me, but I would not really hear or process what he would be saying. This was one of those times.

Therefore, the next morning, as I drove into the parking garage, I was really surprised and annoyed that above the entrance someone had hung a ridiculous heavy sign that slammed into the windshield of the school van. I remember exclaiming out loud disgustedly to the students, "Who would hang a sign so big and so low in the entrance of a parking garage that it could smack into a vehicle? It could have broken the windshield!"

I continued to enter the garage, followed by many early morning vehicles in desperate pursuit of parking, probably to get to work on time. To my astonishment and dismay, I began to encounter low-hanging concrete ceiling beams that scraped the top of the school van, making loud screeching noises that echoed throughout the garage causing garage attendants to come running. This is when I discovered what my husband had been trying to tell me the night before, and this is what the low-hanging sign was trying to warn me about. I found out later that the sign read: "Do NOT ENTER IF YOUR VEHICLE IS THIS HEIGHT." The school van was actually much higher.

The attendants helped me get parked in a safe spot so the students could make it to their test on time. But the problem was going to be getting out of the garage when the test was over. And oh my, it was a problem. First of all, the attendants guided me to the down-ramp that spiraled down to the exit payment booth at ground level. It was no problem going down the ramp to the booth until I reached the bottom and got stuck in the overhang of the payment booth. At this point, I called the school and somehow reached the "always a comedian" Co-op instructor, who just kept loudly laughing and joking about my predicament.

The garage attendants were contemplating letting the air out of the tires to get me loose. Fortunately, I was able to back out from being stuck, but then had to drive in reverse the whole way back up the spiral ramp to the level where I had entered. I would have had difficulty backing up the ramp in my personal little compact car, let alone that big school van. The students, some in fear and some laughing, held on as I kept hitting into the sides of the ramp.

Finally, I reached the entrance floor level. However, to get back to the entrance to be able to exit, I had to encounter those same low-hanging cement beams again. With sparks coming off the top of the van as I screeched under each beam, I was directed to the garage entrance where street traffic had been blocked off in order to allow the school van to exit.

To add to the embarrassment of it all, a special program was being held downtown that day at the museum and multitudes of people were waiting to enter that nearby building. When they realized the street had been blocked, many made their way to see what was happening. And there I was, driving out of the parking garage with sparks and screeching's emanating from the roof of the school van.

The students were now lying on the floor of the van, hiding because they were embarrassed to be seen. It was amazing that any of the students passed their Civil Service Exam that day, but they did. And they had a great story to tell when they got back to school.

Oh yes, when I got back to school, the Autobody shop instructor examined the van and reported that most of the paint had been scraped off the top and that the van would need to be repainted. The Principal, although laughing at me and finding the whole situation humorous, informed me that I would not ever be driving the school van again to any event!

But that is how the Lord enabled me to strike up a great friendship with the Assistant Principal who had asked me to call God on the telephone. He was assigned to drive me whenever I needed to attend any event with my students.

The next year, the Assistant Principal drove me and a group of my students to the Civil Service Exam. I had purchased a small bag of whole peanuts so that he and I could go over to the Harrisburg Capitol Building park and feed the squirrels while the students participated in the exam. We had great theological conversations during the several hours it took for the exam. Sometime within that next year, he began to attend church and was ultimately saved. The following year the Assistant Principal purchased a giant bag of whole peanuts for the squirrels for our next trip.

I must also share the eventual salvation story of another teacher who called upon me to pray for her. Early one morning, she came bursting into my classroom and asked me to pray for her, although she had never before indicated any interest in Christianity. Her husband had left her, and she did not know where to turn or who to turn to. That morning, I prayed with her and continued to meet with her and pray for her whenever she would come to me. Eventually, she was divorced and remarried, and she stopped coming to me for prayer.

Then one afternoon, she came hysterically into my room again asking for prayer, as she had received an emergency call from her daughter's grade school where a man armed with a machete had entered the school and had attacked the Principal and others. Once again, I prayed with her that God would give her peace and safety as she drove to her daughter's school and that God would protect her daughter and others.

Even though this teacher always seemed to come for prayer in desperate situations, she never confessed accepting the Lord as her Savior. But I kept praying for her to get saved.

Fast-forwarding: It had been many years since we taught together at the school. We had not seen one another since I had taken an administrative position at another school, and eventually we had both retired. My husband and I had been invited to a birthday dinner at a restaurant about an hour from our home. As we were leaving the restaurant that afternoon, I passed a table of ladies all wearing red hats. I stopped and commented on how they all looked so nice, and discovered that the teacher was seated among those ladies. It was so nice to see her again. When I inquired about how she had been, she excitedly explained to me how she had accepted the Lord Jesus as her Savior. God is so good! And He is so faithful!

Unfortunately, not all staff relationships and final testimonies turned out to be victorious. One afternoon while the *Youth Alive Club* was conducting their Christian meeting in the school auditorium, which was located at that time up by the administration and business offices, a staff member from one of the offices went out into the hallway and began loudly proclaiming opposition to the service that was being conducted by the club. The students had been singing Christian songs, giving testimonies, preaching, and praying. Because of the location, the staff member could hear most of the service and was totally upset and demanded that at a public school this kind of club should not be allowed to continue. Two weeks later, that staff member died unexpectedly. I do not know if that staff member ever changed and accepted Jesus; I can only pray that overhearing God's Word during our meetings may have reached their heart.

There are other special staff testimonies that I have decided to present in separate chapters of this book that follow, each glorifying the faithfulness and power of our Lord, Jesus Christ. I praise the Lord for His guidance and anointing to reach others through Homeroom 109.

11

They Called It Macaroni!

A time to weep and a time to laugh: a time
to mourn, and a time to dance.
—Ecclesiastes 3:4

Therefore, we are ambassadors for Christ,
God making His appeal through us.
—2 Corinthians 5:20

But in your hearts honor Christ the Lord as holy, always being
prepared to make a defense to anyone who asks you for a reason
for the hope that is in you; yet do it with gentleness and respect.
—1 Peter 3:15

If I had been asked in my early years at the school who the one
person on staff at the school would be that I would probably never
become close friends with, this lady would have immediately come
to my mind. A strikingly gorgeous woman with the sophistication of
a queen. Always a lady, always in control, and always seemingly way
above me in status and maturity.

Although I admit that I felt intimidated and distant from her,
the Lord had placed her and her husband on my heart for several
years, but especially her. They were both strong professionals in their
educational fields. They both served in administrative levels. Yet I felt

in my heart that they were both striving for something that they had not yet attained.

Although I thought I had her all figured out, I discovered over a plate of macaroni that I truly did not know the real "her."

I usually did not eat in the school cafeteria. Most of the time, I would get a tray of food and eat in my classroom, a quiet and peaceful break for me. But for whatever reason, that day, I chose to eat lunch at the faculty table. It sure wasn't because of the menu that day. They served what they called "macaroni." It was some kind of goulash with no flavor. Normally, the food was really good, but not that day.

When I went to be seated at the faculty table that day, there was only one seat available, and it was beside this lady. As I sat down, I could feel that she wasn't thrilled that it was me. To many of the "unbelievers" on staff, I was known as the super religious lady. I found out that her thoughts of me were similar to my thoughts of her: stuffy and arrogant. She would have also added self-righteous to her list on me. So I figured this would be pretty much of a hurry-up-and-eat-and-escape lunch.

When I took my first fork-full of the macaroni, I was sorry I had put it in my mouth. It was awful. I was really hungry. I began to try to doctor it up. I first tried some salt then some pepper. That didn't do it. Then I reached for some ketchup. That only seemed to make it worse. I began looking around the table to see if there might be something there that I could use. It was then that I discovered that she was doing the same thing to her macaroni that I was doing to mine with the same results. In fact, she had been watching me and following me in my remedy choices. I looked at her and defeatedly announced, "Seems like there ain't nothing going to help this stuff!"

With that, we both burst out laughing and began working together to try to "fix" the macaroni. We were like two giddy high school girls, giggling and making sarcastic comments about our food. We tried crazily adding everything and anything we could find, more for the drama of it because we realized that it was to the point of being beyond help. The more things we added, the worse it became, and the more hysterical we became.

We laughed and carried on so loudly that the Principal came over to our table and told us to settle down because we were getting too loud and out of control.

Well, that just set us off even more and brought the Principal back after us a second time, igniting more uncontrollable laughter, now with tears. With the Principal shooting killer looks at us, we got up, took our trays of doctored macaroni to the dumping station, and left the cafeteria and headed for the faculty room. We spent the rest of our lunch period together laughing and sharing our story with any faculty member that entered the room. I don't believe anyone else thought our story was as funny as we did. The most remarkable part to us, though, was that we found out that we were very much alike. We also discovered that we had both misjudged one another.

With our new relationship launched, I really began to seek the Lord to make a way for me to show God's love to my wonderful new friend. God is always faithful.

It was in the fall of the year and several months before Christmas. A faculty member, catching the holiday spirit and wanting to do something to enhance staff morale, presented the idea of having a "Secret Santa" activity for interested staff. The response was strong enough to get the project started. I prayed that the Lord would have me draw someone's name that I could really encourage. I was so excited when I drew my new friend's name!

I had a great time selecting cards, writing notes, and purchasing small gifts for my friend. And I was so blessed when I would hear her share how thrilled she was upon receiving each item. Also, I received so many wonderful, encouraging cards, notes, and gifts from my Secret Santa. I felt like whoever it was really knew me and what I would like.

Instead of ending the project at Christmas, it was decided that it should continue until the end of the school year. A luncheon was scheduled where all the Secret Santas would bring one final gift and reveal their identities. I was so anxious to see the surprise on my friend's face when she would discover that I had been her Secret Santa. Can you imagine both of our faces when it was revealed that we had drawn one another's names! That's how God works!

As our friendship grew stronger, we began to have lunch together regularly. We enjoyed a lot of silly things that we did together, that others would never believe we would do. After all, we were the sophisticated professional and the super religious.

I particularly cherish one time when we ate lunch together in the restaurant of the school's Culinary Arts Program, and for our lunchtime crazy activity, we found ourselves rating the male staff members at the school on a scale of 1–10. We were writing our responses on our napkins and laughing hysterically at our own ratings and comments, agreeing that there was not another male contender that could match our own husbands. Just then my son, a senior at the school, entered the restaurant, came to our table, and asked us what we were doing that we were having so much fun! Yes, we both turned bright red and could not answer him for laughing at ourselves. He just shook his head and left. We agreed that no one in the school would have believed what we were doing!

What a blessing when their son became a Pastor, and they began regularly attending his church. She was such a great mom, always speaking proudly about her son and daughter. I was so honored when she and her husband attended our daughter's wedding, and she told me that it was the most beautiful wedding she ever attended!

We lost touch for a while after I moved on to an administrative position at another school and did not reconnect until after I retired. She and her husband both became interested in the Christian vocational high school that I was working with, especially after one of their closest friends told them that the school had helped their grandson who became the first graduate from the school. They attended many of the programs for the school. Eventually, her husband joined the Advisory Board of the school.

I stand amazed at how God answers prayers so magnificently. Who would have thought that He could even use macaroni!

12

Love the Unlovable

But I tell you, love your enemies and pray
for those who persecute you.

—Matthew 5:44

Hatred stirs up strife: But love covers all sins.

—Proverbs 10:12

But if you love those who love you, what credit is that
to you? For even sinners love those who love them.

—Luke 6:32

There was a teacher at the school that I often felt sorry for because I knew she was a great teacher, but that she was also insecure about her relationships with other staff and particularly the administration. Frequently, she complained that other staff were given privileges and honors and treatment that she never received. She sincerely believed that she was often the target of injustice.

She always worked extra hard to be an outstanding teacher. However, wanting to exemplify her educational abilities, she would sometimes strive with other staff to obtain leadership positions on various educational committees. She and I were not at odds, but we were not friendly either.

One afternoon, at a faculty meeting, she openly and viciously attacked me, right in the middle of the meeting, accusing me of receiving a special privilege that she felt was unfair. She was so upset over the matter that she ended her rant in tears!

I sat there in shock. I had no idea that anyone would be upset over my receiving approval to take several days to attend a technology symposium in Boston, Massachusetts. I was one of those teachers that never left my classes to attend anything. However, I had just assumed the responsibility as the LAN Manager for my computer classroom setup; therefore, when my husband showed me information on a technology symposium that he was scheduled to attend through the company he worked for, I felt it would be beneficial for me to also attend.

I was not getting a free trip. I had not requested that the school cover any of my travel expenses or pay my registration fee. My husband's company was paying all expenses for him to attend, so my transportation was free, as I could ride with him. My hotel bill was only a slight difference of single to double occupancy, which my husband and I personally covered. I also paid for all my own meals and my registration fee to the symposium.

It cost the school, as well as my husband's company, nothing for me to attend. The school did not even need to supply a substitute teacher to cover my classes as the students would remain in their shops on the days I would be away.

However, there was one problem. Often, other teachers were assigned to cover certain class periods or duties for absentee teachers to save on hiring a substitute. In this case, this teacher had been asked to cover one of my duties. She felt her schedule was already overloaded, and that it was unfair to place this burden on her and allow me to go away on a trip with my husband—which is what she perceived it to be, and that really bothered her.

At first, I must admit that I became defensive with her, seeking support from other faculty who comforted me against her attack. But then, the Lord began to work on me to see things His way. Instead of trying to seek revenge and justification, I knew I was to show love and understanding. That is not as easy to do as it sounds.

As the Lord showed me the teacher through His eyes, my mind and heart changed toward her. I was able to understand how overwhelmed she felt having to cover one of my duties with her busy schedule. Therefore, upon my return from the symposium, I thanked her for covering my duty while I was gone and asked her whether there was anything I could do to help her. And actually, she agreed that there was something that I could do for her.

She did not have transportation to the Temple University extension located in downtown Harrisburg, where she was pursuing her Pennsylvania Principal Certification. She needed a way that evening to go to register for her upcoming classes, as her husband was scheduled to be in a meeting after school and could not take her. God certainly weaves an interesting tapestry; He is always at work ahead of me planning my next adventure.

As we traveled together that evening, we talked about our families and our students and found that we had a lot in common. The power of the Lord took over. The enmity between us healed and a new friendship was birthed.

As we neared the university, she excitedly began telling me about the classes that she was taking to obtain her Pennsylvania Principal Certification and suggested that I should take the classes too. She even proposed that we could travel together. I had recently completed my Master of Education degree at Penn State University and was not at all interested in taking more classes to become an administrator, especially a high school Principal.

All the way to the parking garage she kept urging me to consider going for my certification. As I parked the car, she insisted that I go with her to register—just to see the school. Well, I did. It culminated with my introduction to her advisor and my registration for my first two courses! As my friendship with this teacher continued, the Lord orchestrated events to steer it spiritually.

My daughter was a senior at the school that year, and she and I began discussing the possibility of holding a baccalaureate service for her class. The school had never held such a service. So it was decided that I would ask administration if the school, supported by the Christian club, could hold a baccalaureate service for her graduating class.

Because of the "religious" nature of the event, I received an absolute "no" for the school to be involved. However, I was told that I could coordinate the service myself as a parent. It could not be associated with the school and would have to be held off premises.

Immediately, we began planning and organizing the event. I was able to get permission to hold the service at a Methodist Church located across the street from the school. As the parent coordinator, I had flyers distributed to students inviting them and their parents to participate. We received an overwhelming response!

In planning the actual service, we decided to invite other Christian faculty members to participate, and they were excited to do so. Needing someone to play the piano or organ, we found out that my new friend, the teacher, had that gift. I asked her if she would play, and she accepted. She was a bit hesitant, as she told me that she used to play at her church but had not done so for many years. Again, another part of God's tapestry of her life was being created.

The following year, the teacher became interested in the Youth Alive Club and began to visit often. The kids from the group accepted and loved her, and she loved them. Many of these students also attended the Manada Gap Youth Group, where my husband and I were the Youth Leaders. Once, when I had to be at the hospital for an emergency with my husband, the teacher jumped in and covered our youth service for us.

Yes, the Lord worked a miracle in her life that truly became visible to others. She eventually obtained her Pennsylvania Principal Certification and accepted an administrative position at a regular public high school not long before I also obtained my Pennsylvania Principal Certification and took an administrative position at another vocational high school. Ironically, we were able to work together because the public high school where she was the Assistant Principal sent students to the vocational high school where I was Assistant Principal.

Although a devastating event took place shortly thereafter in her life, one that triggered her death, I am comforted believing that she went home to be with the Lord and we will someday be reunited and will rejoice together.

13

—◎—

Not Who You Are—Whose You Are

Therefore whoever confesses Me before men, him I will
also confess before My Father who is in heaven.

—Luke 12:8

Fight the good fight of faith, lay hold on eternal life,
to which you were also called and have confessed the
good confession in the presence of many witnesses.

—1 Timothy 6:12

Choose for yourselves this day whom you will serve, whether
the gods which your fathers served that were on the other side
of the River, or the gods of the Amorites, in whose land you
dwell. But as for me and my house, we will serve the Lord.

—Joshua 24:15

*Each and every day, we make choices. Each and every day we all make a
choice "whom" we will serve that day. We decide under various circumstances if it appears to be more beneficial for us to go the way of the world
rather than to serve the Lord. We look back on what our parents may
have done in the past or what people are doing all around us to justify
our decisions.*

But even if we have made daily decisions in the past to serve the world, we can "choose this day" to serve the Lord. Each and every day we are given a new opportunity to serve Him.

So often we miss the opportunity to be blessed or to bless someone else because we are concerned about how we may look to others and what they may think about us if we respond in obedience to a direction that the Lord gives us.

It was a typical family Thanksgiving dinner at my in-law's. We had the huge dinner early in the afternoon and everyone overate as usual.

My mother-in-law was a wonderful cook. However, my father-in-law was diabetic, so my mother-in-law always tried to bake the holiday pies without sugar or any other kind of suitable sweet replacement. Her pies always looked so inviting, but they tasted so nasty. Every year, I made the same mistake with the pumpkin pie; I would take a full-sized piece. Then I would take the first bite and realize my mistake. I would finish that piece of pie by piling on *Cool Whip* and washing it down with coffee. It was funny to watch the children and my husband make the same mistake and then reach for the *Cool Whip*.

Upon finishing that piece of pie, I was always in misery. I looked forward to completing the cleanup of the dinner dishes so that I could head for a nap on the living room floor. The men would always claim the chairs to watch the televised holiday football game while the women washed the dishes. Therefore, the floor was usually my only nap option. All the grandchildren, who were then in their grade-school years, would go upstairs in the guest bedrooms to play.

So there I was, sound asleep on the living room floor when I heard my children screaming. Immediately, I jumped up to go to their rescue. The problem was, I was not fully awake. My eyes were still closed. I took off running and fell over my brother-in-law who was in the corner lay-back chair. I got back up and took off running again at full speed, this time slamming my shoulder into the archway to the kitchen. I spun around and started up the stairs to the bedrooms. My eyes were finally open, but I was still not fully awake or in control. I kept falling and crawling up the stairs desperately trying to reach my children.

I finally reached the top of the steps and got up and entered the bedroom. All the children were standing there with amazed, confused looks on their faces. I looked wild and beaten up. I was screaming, "Are you okay? Are you okay?" They all answered, "We are okay, are you?"

The ensuing explanation revealed that the children were only playing and the screams that I heard in my sleep were being performed as part of their acting out a pretend drama. The adults that were awake downstairs recognized it as play, but in my sleep, I did not.

When I went back downstairs, I suddenly realized the extent of all my injuries. My knees were brush-burned and bleeding from struggling on the carpet on the steps. My right shoulder really hurt from slamming into the doorway; I could hardly move my arm. My brother-in-law said that he kept thinking that he should have tackled me to stop me to protect me, but I kept going so fast he didn't have a chance. This episode triggered the beginning of problems in my right shoulder that would continue to get worse and worse.

Fast forward: My children were older into their teens. I was teaching at the vocational high school. My busy lifestyle always had me rushing everywhere—to work, to school events, to my children's sporting events and multiple appointments.

My right shoulder had become a hindrance to many of these activities, but it was not bad enough to convince me to see a doctor. That is, not until I was driving to an appointment in a rush, needed something from the back seat behind me, and reached back stretching my right arm way too far. I felt a horrible ripping pain and knew I had finally given the deadly shot to that shoulder. From that point on, it began to throb all the time. I could not sleep at night. It was like having a major toothache in my shoulder.

I finally went to the doctor, and after some tests including an MRI, I was told that I had a torn rotator cuff and would need surgery. As a high school teacher, I knew it would be hard to leave my students and my classes for any extended period of time. Therefore, I did not want to schedule surgery until the summer vacation break. I was desperately trying to make it through until then; however, I was not sleeping at night, and I was thoroughly exhausted from the pain.

One morning I came into school, as usual, totally exhausted and in extreme pain. I took my routine trip to the faculty room before homeroom. The other staff members that were in the faculty room all made comments regarding how awful I looked. I responded with how awful I felt. I then went to my classroom, collapsed at my desk, and sat there wondering how I was going to make it through the day.

Just then, an administrator passed by my room, glanced in, and saw how terrible I looked. The administrator had been a vocational instructor when I began teaching at the school but had received multiple promotions to their current impressive position. As we both had started teaching at the school the same year, we had developed a good friendship, especially since we both confessed Christian beliefs. We often discussed faith topics and shared testimonies.

Entering my classroom, the administrator came over to my desk and asked me what was wrong and if they could do anything. I pathetically shared how much my arm was throbbing and how I had not been sleeping. When asked if I would like prayer, I, of course, responded that I would really appreciate it.

Immediately, the administrator placed hands on my shoulder and began to pray and ask the Lord to heal me and take away the pain. I have to admit that I felt badly because I really did not experience anything miraculous happening during the prayer.

I offered a polite "thank-you" for praying, and then continued explaining how bad my arm had been hurting by trying to demonstrate that I could not even touch my left shoulder with my right hand. To my own amazement, I was able to do it! I could even reach over my head and touch my left shoulder with my right hand. I was unable to do that before the prayer. Then I began moving my arm in a circle, which would have been impossible before the prayer. I began laughing and praising the Lord and loudly proclaiming that I had been healed. That administrator had prayed, and I had been miraculously healed!

I was so excited that I ran next door to the faculty room and began demonstrating my ability to move my arm in every direction, proclaiming to that same group that was there earlier and witnessed me in dire pain that the administrator had prayed for me and God had healed me. I was honestly and completely healed—no pain and full movement! I was celebrating, rejoicing, and praising God! The staff in that faculty room were flabbergasted.

I came back out of that faculty room and headed for the main office. I wanted to share the miracle with everyone in the school. The administrator caught up with me and stopped me, and then said something that totally floored me. I was asked not to tell anyone else that they had prayed for me because it may look bad for them as an administrator to have prayed for a teacher, especially one that was proclaiming that God had healed her.

I could not believe what I was hearing. A miracle had just happened and my Christian friend did not want me to proclaim it for fear of what people would think. This person had come so far in the professional climb to the top and was apprehensive that my testimony might jeopardize their future.

We are now both retired from the public school system. I spoke with my friend recently, and we finally talked about what happened that day. My friend told me how sorry and embarrassed they now are about denying God then.

We all have been there. Peter was there. We all have failed and have been overtaken by the world's way of causing us to think or act. But each day we are given the opportunity to start again and make our choice. Choose "this day" whom you will serve. Forgiveness is there for the past days. Strength and encouragement are there for victory for each new day.

14

Stay On the Bus

Therefore you shall be careful to do as the Lord
your God has commanded you; you shall not
turn aside to the right hand or to the left.
—Deuteronomy 5:32

Therefore, my beloved brethren, be steadfast, immovable,
always abounding in the work of the Lord, knowing
that your labor is not in vain in the Lord.
—1 Corinthians 15:58

In the educational field, teachers and administration are usually required to obtain continuing education credits to maintain their current certifications. I, therefore, chose to go for a Master of Education degree to obtain these required credits while I was teaching. I enrolled at Penn State University in the Training and Development program and graduated with a dual degree that added Public Personnel Administration to my resume (I still do not know why I obtained this additional degree as I have never needed or used it).

I attended classes in the evenings and would leave immediately after school, usually zipping through a drive-through for some chicken nuggets for dinner. This schedule was very demanding, as I juggled studying time and my teaching responsibilities with my family obligations and desires. I know it was only by the strength of the Lord that I was able to accomplish everything. I also know that I was following the Lord's direction for what He was preparing me to eventually do years later.

As I was sitting at a desk on the first evening of a new course at the college and was observing the other adult students entering the classroom, a fairly tall African-American lady entered the room wearing a head-covering and a long-skirted dress. While I continued watching her, the Lord impressed to me that she was going to become one of my best friends!

I admit that I was skeptical of what I felt I was hearing from God. This lady and I appeared to be total opposites as far as I could tell. I was not concerned that we contrasted in height and race, but more apparently and divisively, she appeared to be Muslim. I wondered how in the world we could become best friends.

Then, to my amazement, after walking to the other side of the room, she circled back, came over and sat down at a desk next to me. There were other desks available, yet she sat right down beside me.

The class started, as most do, with the professor distributing and reviewing the syllabus. The class was dismissed with the professor announcing the requirement that everyone must purchase the textbook immediately and enforced the directive by giving an extensive reading assignment to be completed for the next scheduled class.

This is when I took notice that the lady next to me did not have a textbook with her. Initiating a conversation, I asked if she had her textbook or was going to the school bookstore after class to get one. She told me that she was probably not going to get the textbook until the following week. That is when the Lord spoke to my heart again and told me to write a check for $50 and offer it to her to buy the textbook.

I asked her to wait a moment, that I had something for her. Obediently, I quickly took out my checkbook and wrote the check, leaving the name blank as I did not even know her name at the time. Expecting her to be acceptable and blessed by the offer, I was surprised when she, instead, became angry and offended. I certainly did not mean to offend her, and I was really confused by why God had me make the offer. I was worried that my direction may not have come from Him.

She defensively asked me why I would offer her the check. All I felt I could honestly do was admit to her that I felt that the Lord had spoken to my heart and directed me to do it. I apologized that I had apparently insulted her and said that I was just trying to be obedient to the Lord. It was obvious that she was surprised that I mentioned the Lord to her, a Muslim. Oh no, did I add another insult to the injury!

Instead of becoming angrier with me, which I expected her to do, she smiled. She asked me my name, and I told her to call me Sandy. Then she, mispronouncing my first name as she has continued to do throughout the time I have known her, said, "Sanny, I will accept your check and use it to get my textbook." She then gave me her name, and I entered it on the check. I gave her the check, and to my amazement, we hugged and she thanked me.

The next class she arrived with her textbook, sat next to me again, and asked to be on my team when the professor directed us to form into teams to complete the project assignments for the course. Needing transportation from her home to class later in the course, I began to pick her up and transport her home. Amazingly, as God had revealed to me, we became great friends.

As my life was centered in Jesus, through our church, the youth group that I led, my students at school and involvement with the school's Christian club, I could not help but talk a lot about all these things with her. And as time went on, she shared her history with me. She had been raised in Philadelphia and had attended an Assembly of God church with her family when she was growing up. She never told me why she eventually left that faith to marry into the Muslim religion.

I completed my courses at Penn State University and graduated and thought that probably we would only connect now and then by phone to continue our friendship. However, to my surprise, as I was teaching in my classroom one morning, I saw her go by in the hallway. Later, I saw her at lunch and found out that she had obtained a job as a Teaching Assistant at our school. We were now working together!

To the curiosity of many staff members at the school, the labeled *crazy Christian lady* and the obvious Muslim lady continued an amazing friendship for the next several years. We ate lunch together when possible and hung out together on staff in-service days.

One of the funniest stories happened to us on an in-service day. It involved us and the Assistant Principal, a young man who was known as the prankster of the staff. He was especially proud of all the tricks he would play on the teachers. He would obnoxiously boast about how no one was ever able to pull off a prank on him, including all the friends in his dorm at college. Although unplanned, we were soon to destroy that claim and take him down big time!

Dress-down attire was permitted on in-service days, so on that particular day I wore jeans and a pullover sweatshirt that my sister-in-law had bought me for Christmas. The shirt was green and had a giant *Tigger the Tiger* on the front of it. As a child, I did not like the *Winnie the Pooh* cartoons and did not watch them. I honestly was not familiar with who *Tigger* was or what he was known as. But I did like the shirt.

My friend and I had just gone to the cafeteria to get our lunch and were heading for the faculty room to eat. I was carrying my tray out in front of me and was kind of walking with a bounce, as I was in my sneakers. The Assistant Principal came up the hall passing us on his way to the cafeteria. As he passed us, he looked straight at the front of my sweat-shirt and laughingly and loudly remarked, "Do all Tiggers bounce?"

I know my face turned red. I turned to my friend and, embarrassed and offended, asked her if I had heard him right regarding what I could not believe he just said. Discovering that I knew nothing about the *Tigger* cartoon character, she began to laugh hysterically, realizing how I had taken the remark personally. She explained to me about the cartoon and the phrase that he had used, trying to defend what the Assistant Principal had meant. She assured me that he was not being disrespectful or perverted, as I though he was. We both could not stop laughing as we entered the faculty room.

The school Psychologist and the lead Guidance Counselor, both ladies, just happened to already be eating lunch in the faculty room. They were naturally curious about why we were laughing so hard, and we told them about how I had misinterpreted what the Assistant Principal had said. They, too, found our story to be hilarious.

Then we all got an idea. With both ladies, the Psychologist and the Guidance Counselor, serving on the Sexual Harassment Committee, we decided to work together to set up the Assistant Principal.

After lunch, I went back to my classroom and called the Assistant Principal from my classroom telephone. When he answered, I informed him that I was very disappointed in him regarding his insulting and perverted remark that he had made to me. I told him that I was old enough to be his mother and was really surprised that he would speak to me that way. All the while he tried to explain that he had nieces and nephews that he watched cartoons with and that he was only quoting *Tigger the Tiger*. I told him that I had already reported his conduct to the Sexual Harassment Committee consisting of the school Psychologist and the lead Guidance Counselor, and they both recommended that I complete a formal complaint against him.

He began pleading with me and tried in every way to convince me that his remark was innocent. I told him that I would be meeting again with the school Psychologist and the lead Guidance Counselor and would call him back. I waited about five minutes and called him back. I then told him that we had all just spoken together and we decided to let him know that he had just really been *pranked* by the best of us. The telephone went quiet and he hung up.

Several minutes later, the Administrative Director of the school came to my room, gave me a high-five, and congratulated me on a prank well done! He said that the Assistant Principal came out of his office pure white and looked like he was going to pass out. He also said that they never would have suspected me to be the one to get him—not the good Christian lady!

My new best friend and I continued to have a lot of fun together and our differences managed to somehow blend us together. She even visited with me at my home. She was not permitted to remove her head covering in front of a man, but when my husband was not around, she was allowed to remove it, and she did. I would help her color and wash and fix her hair.

I never gave up my stand for Christ around her and she always defended her position as the wife of a Muslim husband. In recent years, as I was developing a Christian vocational high school, she contacted me to discuss the possibility of including Muslim students. However, she recommended that I not require them to attend any Christian-related services or teachings. They should only attend for the vocational training.

I strongly rejected her proposal, stating that God had called me to create a Christian vocational high school, with emphasis on evangelism. Every student attending would need to agree to attend Chapel every day and complete all Christian-related assignments. All curriculum would be Biblically-integrated.

She answered me, saying, "Sanny, that's what I like most about you. You get on the bus, and you stay on the bus!"

15

He Showed Me Her Hurts

I will never leave you nor forsake you.
—Hebrews 13:5

Cast your care upon Him, for He cares for you.
—1 Peter 5:7

In-service days were not my favorite days as a teacher, and I believe many other teachers would agree with me. Usually, I would have so much additional work to do with grading and reports and curriculum, that I really wanted to use an in-service day just to catch up. The last thing I wanted to do was to listen to a speaker or participate in team activities.

Teachers are usually not good students and often can be a speaker's worst audience. When I became an administrator, I saw this from the other side and tried to do my best to make in-service days productive for the teachers as well as meet their ongoing training needs.

Well, there I was, as a teacher, in one of those in-service days. It was lunchtime, and fortunately, vocational schools recognized that feeding teachers and staff well on in-service days made the day go much better. The lunch break provided an opportunity to change the stress of the day, as most of the teachers and staff members would sit together, relax, and fellowship and get into a refreshed state of mind for the afternoon activities.

Sitting with several teachers and staff members who were also believers, we were sharing various stories, many Christian-centered. A staff member, who was not a part of our regular group, came over with us to sit as there was no room at other tables.

This person was known to be a very outspoken individual, especially against Christianity. She was married to a Muslim. Knowing she would be uncomfortable with any spiritual conversation, we avoided such with her joining us. One by one everybody finished eating and left the table to go to put some time into their classrooms. Eventually, it was just her and I at the table.

Praying intently that God would give me an opportunity to effectively, yet lovingly, be able to witness to her, God brought to my memory a young girl that I had prayed with at the altar of our church at a youth service over five years before. The young girl came to our youth service only that one time. She had been invited by and came with a friend who regularly attended. That evening, as I prayed with the young teen, she told me that she wanted to trust God but shared that her father had been a Pastor of a church and had sexually abused her. We prayed together and cried together. After the service, she needed a way home, so she guided me and I personally took her to where she lived. That was the first and last time I ever saw her.

Wondering why God gave me that memory at that moment, He spoke to my heart that the young girl I had prayed with at that altar was that staff member's daughter. There was no way, other than God telling me, that I would have known this.

God also revealed to me that the staff member was angry at God for what her former husband, who was supposed to have been a Pastor representing God, had done to her daughter and to her. She had turned against God and relinquished her faith because of it. This explained her current marriage to a Muslim and her acceptance of that religion.

Wow! I knew that God wanted me to present this to her. So I asked her if she had an older daughter that would be in her late teens or early twenties and she said that she did and asked me why I asked her this. I then described how the girl looked over five years ago and asked if her daughter looked like that. She said that she did and now she really wanted to know why I was asking her these things. I then described the house and its location where I took the girl home and asked if she lived there at that time. She was now really amazed and asked how I knew all this.

I then revealed to her that God had just shown me all this for me to share with her. I explained to her how her daughter had attended the youth group only once over five years before. I told her how we prayed together and what her daughter had shared with me. She was really in shock!

Then God had me tell her that He still loved her and wanted her to know that He had never left her. Her eyes filled up, and she said that she had to go and she left the table.

I never had another chance to speak with her. I believe that she purposely avoided me, but I knew that God used that opportunity to vividly let her know that He was still there for her and always would be. I could only pray that she would stop rejecting His love and accept it and, once again, trust the Lord to help her and heal her.

Often, when we are hurting and God seems like He has deserted us, it is so hard to keep on believing. However, if we continue to trust Him, He will get us through anything we are facing. I know the Lord will always make a way for you and for me.

16

Adding My Two Cents

Therefore to him that knoweth to do good,
and doeth [it] not, to him it is sin.

—James 4:17

Speak the truth in love.

—Ephesians 4:15

Unfortunately, not every faculty or staff relationship that I have experienced has been pleasant resulting in a positive testimony, especially in the case of the situation I am now going to share.

I have always believed that when a teacher or school staff member does not perform professionally to the detriment of a student, responsibility should be to defend the student, not the job or position of the teacher or the staff member. We are to be there for the students; they are the reason we have a job. We should not be protecting the jobs of staff members who knowingly and deliberately do not professionally perform their duties, especially when it results in damaging the learning process or safety of students.

With that stated, I will present the situation. A substitute teacher who was known to have difficulty with classroom management had been placed in a long-term assignment in an academic classroom. Students were often heard discussing episodes of conflict with the teacher, many describing how the teacher consistently argued with them, threatened them, and bullied them. Administration was receiving an unusually large number of student disciplinary referrals from the teacher on a daily basis, indicative of a combative instead of cooperative learning environment that had been created.

Academic classes were clustered according to shops in order to integrate academics according to trade requirements. The particular trade cluster served by this academic class consisted predominately of male students. As all trades were required to take my course, I had many of the students who were in the academic class as students in my class, so I overheard a lot of the complaints from these students and a lot of the war stories.

It was close to Spring Break, and I was looking forward to my daughter coming home from college for a visit. As I would also have some days off for the Easter holiday, I anticipated spending as much time as possible with her. However, I was to become involved in a situation of defending a student that would cut into that precious time.

Some students had begun to retaliate against the substitute teacher. Actually, it was revealed that full classes of students would actually plot together to pull various pranks just to annoy and aggravate.

As the teacher turned to write on the blackboard (yes, we used them back then), one particular group of students threw pennies, some hitting the teacher's back and others hitting the chalkboard. The substitute teacher reported the incident as a physical attack, and the administration began to pursue it as such.

The substitute teacher went so far as to leave school and go to the emergency room, claiming to have suffered trauma, hoping to substantiate the claim of physical attack. The teacher even stated that they could have suffered being knocked unconscious by one of the pennies that hit their head, although no physical marks or injuries indicated such force took place.

As administration began the shake-down of questioning the students from the class, all of the students denied throwing a penny—except for one. One young man, a great young man raised by a Christian mom and brought up through the church, desiring to be honest, admitted that he had thrown a penny. When questioned about who else threw a penny, the young man stated that he would not "rat" on anyone else.

Therefore, desiring to make an example of the student to other students, administration decided to prosecute that one student for the crime of attacking a faculty member, with the heavy penalty of being expelled from the school for the remainder of the year and placed back into his sending school district with no hope of being accepted back at the vocational school to complete his trade education.

This young man had been a model student in his shop and always a pleasant, respectful, and eager student in my classroom. I could not allow the vindictive motives of the substitute teacher and the administration to ruin the hopes and dreams of a student who exemplified honesty over the other students in his class. This student could have chosen to lie, just like the other students, and would have received no penalty. How unjustified!

The charges for expulsion were filed by administration against the student and a hearing before the school Board was scheduled over the Spring Break. I decided that I must step forward and testify on behalf of the character of the student and the unfairness of the charge, even if it meant giving up time with my daughter.

To the aggravation of the Principal and the resentment of the substitute teacher, I did show up before the school board to testify on behalf of the student. The Principal, playing the part of the prosecutor, came at me hard and nasty. The Lord was faithful to give me the right answers and calmness to successfully defend the student and sway the decision to only suspend the student for three weeks and allow him to return to his shop, complete the year, with permission to complete his trade program at the school.

I look back and thank the Lord that I showed up to defend the student. The student returned after his suspension and continued as a model student up until his following birthday.

You see, I entered school that morning to sign in and pick up my mail, and I heard the secretaries discussing a tragic event that happened to one of our students. I asked what they were talking about, and they told me that the student that I had defended had been killed in an automobile accident the night before on his birthday.

17

Standing in the Classroom

For we wrestle not against flesh and blood, but against
principalities, against powers, against the rulers of the darkness
of this world, against spiritual wickedness in high places.
—Ephesians 6:12

To open their eyes, so that they may turn from darkness to light and
from the power of Satan to God, that they may receive forgiveness
of sins and an inheritance among those sanctified by faith in Me.
—Acts 26:18

Therefore take up the full armor of God, so that when
the day of evil comes, you will be able to stand your
ground, and having done everything, to stand.
—Ephesians 6:13

It was the beginning of the class period and I was standing in front
of the classroom taking attendance. The students had "logged in" on
their computers and were intensely concentrating on their typing. I
was not expecting the horrifying vision that God sent to me that day.

As I looked up from my gradebook, completing the attendance,
all of a sudden, flames of fire shot up encircling every student's desk,
trapping them where they each sat. They were individually engulfed
in the flames and could not get away from their desks to escape.

They were stretching out their arms to me and screaming hysterically, "Help, me, Mrs. Cook, please help me!"

That vision lasted only a few seconds, but it tremendously altered my viewpoint of the fullness of my ministry responsibility throughout my remaining career in public education. It defined my calling more fully, prompting me to realize that I had been placed by God in the high school and anointed by God to open the eyes of my students so that they would turn from darkness to light and from the power of Satan to God. So many of our high school teens, then and now, are being held in bondage through being personally targeted by the power of Satan. These precious students are headed for the fiery flames of Hell if we, as Christians, do not go to war for them.

The power of darkness was aggressively invading this school and spiritual warfare had become very real in my classroom. Several of my male students openly identified themselves as Satanic high priests. One of these young boys lived in a little town over the mountain from my home, and I was familiar with his residential location. Students from our youth group told me that they heard that the garage/shed behind his house was being used as a Satanic meeting place where animal sacrifices were being performed. Although I never heard that it was confirmed, I would get a creepy feeling every time I drove by the location.

Two young girls who had been dating the boys described above came to me one Wednesday afternoon and asked if they could attend our church youth group service that evening. They acted desperate, insinuating that they were in some kind of danger, and stated that they wanted help.

It was common knowledge at the school that a group of students would wait for me after school on Wednesdays and ride with me to our church youth service. The girls asked urgently if they could meet me after school and ride along with us to the service that evening. I assured them that I was really glad that they wanted to attend and that I would be happy to take them along with our group that afternoon. Unfortunately, even though we waited quite a while for them, neither girl showed up to meet us after school and neither showed up for the church youth service that night.

The next day at school, I saw the girls' names on the morning absentee list. I inquired at the school office about the girls and was told that they both had been taken to the hospital emergency room the night before because they had been physically attacked. I found out later that both girls had viciously suffered having a Satanic pentagram carved into their stomachs with a razor knife. I continued in prayer for the girls, but they never came back to see me. I was told that they had been horribly threatened and were scared to even come near my classroom.

Giving glory to God, even though the power of darkness was evident at the school, the power of God was more evident. There were several specific instances where I became involved, although not intentionally, in episodes of spiritual warfare, where God arose and His enemies were scattered!

As I was walking through the hallway one afternoon heading to another area of the school, I passed one of the young boys involved in the Satanic cult. I began to pray inside myself (not audibly) in the Spirit. The demonic spirit within the boy reacted, causing him to scream and growl at me, like he wanted to attack me. I remember the evil that I could see deep in his eyes.

Other students in the hallway were confused by what was happening as they were wondering why that student began acting so aggressively toward me. They had observed that I had not said anything or had not done anything to him. But I knew what had triggered it. I just kept on walking away from the student and praying, leaving him behind in the hallway.

Oftentimes in my classroom, as I would take attendance, I would silently pray for each student as I marked them "present" or "absent." It was never obvious to anyone that I was praying, as I always did so silently, inside me.

However, one day, I encountered a surprising retaliation when I began to pray silently in the Spirit for a student that I sensed had a major problem. The student sprung up from his desk in a rage and picked up his chair to throw at me. I had not said anything to him, I was just silently taking attendance and praying.

Fearing for the safety of the other students, I quickly ordered all of them to evacuate my room, and they immediately went running out into the hallway. I then commanded, in the name of Jesus, that the young man not come near me. He turned and threw the chair across the classroom, away from me. All the while I kept praying in the Spirit, now out loud, and all the while he kept cursing me.

Praise the Lord, several of the students ran up to the school office, got the Assistant Principal, who arrived with help and took him out of my classroom.

Then there was the instance of the divine tackle. It was the last period of the day, right before the afternoon announcements were to come on followed by dismissal. For some reason, only three students were in attendance for the class. Two of the students were girls whose seats were up front in the first row of the classroom near my desk, and the other student was a boy in the first seat in the last row, across the room from us.

As the girls shut down their computers, preparing for dismissal, they began talking out loud to one another, discussing descriptive vulgar details of their dating lives that they apparently wanted me to overhear. It was evident that they wanted to trigger a response from me, which they did. I left them know that I was offended by their conversation, but even more, I was concerned about their ungodly lifestyles that they were sharing and about how their futures could suffer because of it. I told them both that I cared about them, and more importantly, God loved them, no matter what they were doing.

At that point, one of the girls began asking me questions about God, so I answered her questions as best as I could. She then indicated that she wanted to attend the Christian club at the school and also that she was interested in the youth group at the church.

This setoff the young man on the other side of the room, who stood to his feet and yelled at me that I should not be speaking to students about God at the school. As he continued to threaten that he was going to report me to administration, all of a sudden, he fell flat down on the floor on his back. I got up from my desk to get to him to see if he was okay, but he jumped up and ran out of the classroom. The dismissal bell rang and the day was over.

The next day, he came to my room. I thought he was coming because he was still upset with me. However, he immediately started to apologize to me for yelling at me the day before. He said that while he was yelling at me, something grabbed him by his shoulders, lifted him up and slammed him to the floor on his back. He knew that there was no one over by his desk. He was a fairly big guy and it would have taken a large, strong person to do that. He said that he believed that God had sent an angel that slammed him to the floor for yelling at me. He then stated that he wanted to come to the next Christian club meeting! Ultimately, both he and the girl with the questions from that class eventually came to the club meetings, and both accepted the Lord. The next testimony describes this young man's salvation experience.

In 1988 an Assembly of God Church in Radcliff, Kentucky, experienced a tragic bus accident killing three of their pastoral staff and twenty-four children. The church had sponsored a trip to King's Island near Cincinnati on May 14. On the trip home, the bus carrying sixty-seven children and adults was struck by a drunken driver going northbound in the southbound lanes of the interstate. It became one of the worst drunken driving crashes in US history.

The wife of the Pastor of that church, Evangelist Martha Tennison, began traveling throughout the country sharing the testimonies from the crash and emphasizing God's faithfulness especially in times of tragedy. She came to the Harrisburg area, and the Lord miraculously arranged for her to present her message through the Christian club at the school to any student at the school that wanted to attend!

Because our Youth Alive Club was now permitted to advertise events, students who were not regular club members were able to obtain a pass to attend the presentation that was held in the auditorium of the school. That large auditorium was packed that afternoon for the presentation. At the end of her message, Evangelist Tennison gave an altar call, and students all over the auditorium stood up to accept the Lord. We actually have a video of that service!

Just before the altar call, a student raised his hand and asked if he could speak. It was the young man that said he had been tackled by an angel in my classroom. He stood before the other students in the auditorium and gave the complete testimony of what happened to him that afternoon and urged other students to believe that God is real. He also stood along with many other students that afternoon to receive salvation.

The girl that I described who had the questions in the class who got saved, later invited a Vietnamese student from her shop program to our church youth group that she began attending. The Vietnamese student and his siblings all attended the vocational school and were known by their story of how they escaped from Vietnam in a small boat and were rescued out in the ocean.

The Vietnamese boy finally did agree to attend the youth service, but made it clear to everyone that he did not believe in God and was only there to satisfy his friend's ongoing request to attend. The youth service opened with greeting and prayer and went into praise and worship, except the worship began as literally nothing more than "singing" songs.

I stopped the service. The young man was sitting in the front pew. The regular youth group members had been standing to sing, but he had remained seated and was not singing. I didn't blame him. During the worship, many of the youth were passing photos and notes, distracting one another, or just merely singing.

I admit I went into a rant. I blasted the whole group. How was the invited guest to believe that God was real when the group who was supposed to believe that God is real was not worshipping in Spirit or in truth to bring God's presence into the service?

Then we started over in praise and worship. This time the members of the youth group really began to worship God, raising their hands and their hearts in true praise. All of a sudden, I looked down at the front pew and the young Vietnamese guest was lying face down on the pew sobbing! The Lord came into that service and revealed Himself to that young man.

Finally, I will share about the girl that we took into our home during her senior year. She was going to try to leave her home because her mother's boyfriend began living with them and she was frustrated with what was going on around her. She was a brilliant student with a great personality and a craving for the things of God. I offered to take her in and get her through her final year of school.

Many amazing things took place to strengthen her faith while she lived with us. One of the most memorable was when she was with me downtown in the city late on a summer's night. We were on our way home from an event, and I had to stop at a bank to get cash out of the MAC machine.

As we pulled into the drive-through at the bank, everything was dark and deserted except for the light illuminating the MAC machine. I pulled up to it and put in my card and began punching in the code and numbers to get my cash.

Suddenly, two men came up to our car, one on either side at our windows which were down. We were alone in the car, both sitting up front. It was obvious that we were going to be robbed and possibly physically attacked.

As the men leaned in both our windows arrogantly toward each of us, they suddenly became distracted by something in the back seat of the car. As I said, we were alone in the car and there was nothing in the back seat. The look on both of their faces went from puzzled to fearful to shock to open-mouthed fright! They both shrieked and ran from the car like they were running for their lives.

We both turned to look in the back to see what it was that they obviously saw—but there was nothing in the back seat. I then retrieved my bank card and money from the machine and we sped out of there.

The Lord must have placed some nasty-looking angels or something in that back seat that scared those men away. We praised God and laughed as we talked about how funny the men's scared faces looked. We knew that God had miraculously protected us that evening.

18

Are You in a Rock Video?

Be sober, be vigilant; because your adversary the devil walks
about like a roaring lion, seeking whom he may devour.

—1 Peter 5:8

Beloved, do not believe every spirit, but test the spirits,
whether they are of God; because many false prophets have
gone out into the world. By this you know the Spirit of
God: Every spirit that confesses that Jesus Christ has come
in the flesh is of God, and every spirit that does not confess
that Jesus Christ has come in the flesh is not of God.

—1 John 4:1

Ye are of God, little children, and have overcome them: because
greater is He that is in you, than he that is in the world.

—1 John 4:4

Finally, my brethren, be strong in the Lord and in the power
of His might. Put on the whole armor of God, that you may
be able to stand against the wiles of the devil. For we do not
wrestle against flesh and blood, but against principalities,
against powers, against the rulers of the darkness of this age,
against spiritual hosts of wickedness in the heavenly places.

—Ephesians 6:10–18

You shall make them as a fiery oven in the time of
Your anger; The Lord shall swallow them up in
His wrath, And the fire shall devour them.

—Psalm 21:9

Those that choose to serve the powers of darkness have chosen for themselves an eternity in Hell's flames. The devil will be unable to reward those who served him, as he will be in chains together with those that served him. He does not win and rule. God is the winner! God has empowered us to win, but we must be spiritually prepared for the battle so that we can go into the battle and win. And remember, what is meant by the devil for evil, God will mean it for good. (Genesis 50:20)

It was in the spring of 1994 and the Penn-Del Assembly of God Youth Convention was scheduled and soon to take place over Spring Break on Easter weekend. The convention was being held in Pittsburgh, Pennsylvania.

Manada Gap Youth Group was energized and looking forward to the convention. Because my teaching schedule enabled me to teach every tenth-grader at the vocational high school, and because I could advertise upcoming events through our Christian club to my classes, I began to post advertisements on our club bulletin board so every class would know about the event.

My husband and I decided that we would cover all but $10 of the registration expenses for any new guest youth that decided to attend. Students began inviting other students and we ended up having a total of sixty youth attend the event through our youth group.

That weekend we loaded a school bus and a van with students and chaperones and headed to Pittsburgh for the convention. We had a lot of new youth attending; many of them were not Christians and some had never attended a church service. We were excited to think of the salvation possibilities that we could be blessed with.

When we arrived in Pittsburgh, we discovered that the Penn-Del Convention had three major hotels booked with kids. We also found out that three major *Rock Groups* had arrived in town, intentionally to crash the convention. They were spread out in all three hotels. *Pantera* was one of the groups and *Great White* was another. I don't recall the name of the third group. I remember *Great White* only because I stepped on one of the members of the group accidently on an elevator. One of my students exclaimed, "Mrs. Cook, you just stepped on Great White!" And my response was, "A great white what?" Through the following testimony, documented by YouTube references, you will know why I remember *Pantera*.

The Penn-Del Youth Convention was phenomenal. The theme for that year was *Youth-Quake*. There were great speakers, great worship groups and musicians, great activities, great workshops, and great food. However, there was little sleep, especially for the leaders and advisors.

Throughout the event, I was unaware of the outreach to our kids that was taking place by the rock groups. They were propping their hotel room doors open and inviting our youth to visit. We were also unaware that they had mounted video cameras above their beds, and they were taping our youth. In many cases, they were taping sessions with them where they were mocking them by playing "religious mind games" with them to make them look foolish, especially when they placed them in awkward positions of defending their Christian beliefs.

On the last morning of the trip, we were up very early loading the bus to head back to Harrisburg. I ultimately discovered that a number of our youth were missing, including my daughter. One of our younger youth leaders said that she knew where they were. She told me that they were in *Dimebag Darrell's* hotel room witnessing to him. I asked who he was and she told me that he was part of the *Pantera* rock group that was in our hotel. I asked her to lead me to where they were.

Sure enough, when I arrived at the room, the door was propped open with a shoebox. I listened and heard the students in the room, so I opened the door. The kids all announced me as their Youth

Leader and Dimebag invited me into his room. I declined the offer and told the kids that the bus was loaded and it was time to leave. They all began begging me to come in and told me that Dimebag wanted to hear more about Jesus. And then he added that he really wanted to meet me.

I was so extremely exhausted from the weekend excitement coupled with very little sleep. I just wanted to go home. But I looked at their faces and realized that I was always teaching them to take every opportunity to witness, and I was not modeling that for them at that moment. Therefore, feeling guilty and convicted, I entered the room.

Exhausted, and not impressed, I sat down on the bottom of Dimebag's bed. He was sitting up in bed by his pillow. I began with, "Okay, so what did you want to talk about?" The kids began to tell me all at once that he had been telling them he was a Christian and that he believed in Jesus. And to that he added, "Yes, Mama, that's right. I am a Christian too and I believe in Jesus."

Even though I was physically and mentally tired, suddenly the Spirit of God came over me, stood me up, and I spun around and asked him boldly, "If you are a Christian and you believe in Jesus, who do you say Jesus is?" I knew this was from God and not me because I was too tired to come up boldly with any kind of a response.

His answer confirmed that he did not believe in Jesus as the Son of God. He said that it was all relative and that many people believe in the man named Jesus in different ways. I told him he was right and that even the devil believes in Jesus and trembles. But I also told him that he has to confess that Jesus is the Christ, the Son of the Living God, in order to defend that he is a believer. He could not do that.

The conversation became more intense as Dimebag shared that he was demon-possessed and that he did not believe he could be set free. He said that even though he had a lot of money and fame, it was all useless to him because he had no control over his own life.

I asked him to allow me to pray for him to be set free, but he refused to take my hand and he backed up into the corner of his bed and crouched like a scared animal. I tried to pursue him, and it was at that time that my husband, Randy, and the other Youth Leader, Fred, entered the room.

Randy was the driver for the bus and Fred was the driver for the van that transported us to Pittsburgh. They were both loading up to head home and realized that some of the kids were missing and that I was missing. They asked if anyone knew where we were, and they were told that we were somewhere in the hotel in a room with one of the members of the *Pantera* rock group.

Randy and Fred entered the hotel with no idea where to look for us. They approached the elevator and the doors opened and they got on. They did not push any button choosing a floor, as they did not know what floor to choose. The elevator doors closed and the elevator went up to the eleventh floor. The elevator stopped and the doors opened. Therefore, Randy and Fred got off on the eleventh floor. They walked back the hallway and heard our voices, as the door to Dimebag's room was still open.

Randy entered the room first, planning to announce that the bus was waiting and that we needed to leave. Instead, he entered the room, grunted loudly, and bent over as though he had been punched really hard in the stomach, straightened back up, and with a booming voice, he commanded, "I am telling you right now, out of here! You are casting pearls before swine and I will not allow this. Leave now!" We all began to exit the room and Randy continued to prophesy to Dimebag. Through Randy God spoke that their group should take their damnation elsewhere and added that Dimebag and his camera would rot in the Hell that he had chosen for himself. After we were all out in the hallway leaving, God spoke again through Randy and instructed all of us to "cleanse ourselves off, for we had been in the presence of evil."

Okay, I was wide awake now. And so were most of the people on that floor in the hotel. Doors were open everywhere, and people were watching from their rooms in amazement at the episode taking place in the hallway. Dimebag was now screaming obscenities at us as we departed down the hallway.

We all headed back to the bus and the van, none of us speaking a word. We were all in shock over what just took place. We had been in the midst of a battle between Heaven and Hell.

Randy drove the bus to the first rest stop along the highway and he pulled in. He built a fire at one of the grill pits and instructed everyone to burn autographs and anything else associated with the rock groups. We gathered around the fire and prayed and asked for cleansing and protection from what we had experienced.

It was the quietest ride back home with youth that I have ever experienced.

That evening we began to get telephone calls from some of the youth that were in that room. One young man called in the middle of the night and said that "spirits" were flying through his bedroom and asked me to pray for him.

This was my first real encounter in any kind of face-to-face combat with demonic power. I admit that I did not know what I was doing. I just wanted to take charge and see Dimebag get freed. What I did not realize, and what God later showed me, was that I put some of our youth in that room in danger. Some of them were not saved and the demonic power could have attacked them. I prayed for forgiveness and asked for greater wisdom to minister to those youth.

I called the leader of the Penn-Del Youth ministry and told him what had happened. His answer to me was that he was extremely tired from the Convention and was not interested in pursuing some kind of witch hunt, and that I should not make any kind of deal out of it.

The next week at school, our youth were sharing the story. Many of my classes were asking me to tell them about it. I would always let them know that if I answered their questions, it was going to be an answer that described something God was doing. I would add that if anyone in the class did not wish to hear the answer, I would not give it and would speak only to the ones with the questions at another time and place. In most cases, everyone always wanted to hear the story. Some listened but did not believe me.

One young man who did not believe the story personally discovered later that it was true. The following summer during school break I ran into him at a neighborhood shopping center. He came up to me and excitedly reported that he knew I wasn't lying about the *Pantera* story. He said that the *RIP* magazine had run an article featuring *Pantera* and that they were talking about the "Youth Quakers" who came into their hotel room in Pittsburgh. That Sunday, the young man and his girlfriend come to our church and ended up at the altar accepting Jesus as their Savior.

The following year at school, several students approached me at lunchtime as I was returning my food tray and asked me if I was in a rock video. I laughed and sarcastically answered, "Sure, I am the lead guitar player." They were really serious and urged me to listen to them. They told me that they saw me in a rock video. They said it was the new rock video by *Pantera*.

They now had my full attention. I asked them the name of the video, and they told me it was called *Vulgar Video*.

It was winter, and there was snow and ice on the ground. But in spite of the bad roads, I sent our son, Braden, out into the weather that evening on a mission to find and purchase that video. He successfully and safely returned with the video.

It was awful having to scan through that video, almost to the end, trying to find where we were on that video. The segment we were in was themed demonic. The camera mounted above Dimebag's bed had filmed our entire encounter with him that morning. Much of that encounter was included in the video, although it was slanted to make fun of us and make us look like we had attacked them.

Satan meant this for evil. But God turned it around for good. Each year that I continued to teach at the Votech, the first day of classes, *every* class would ask me if I was in a *Pantera* video. And each time I was able to share the testimony of God's power against the demons of Hell. Through this testimony, many students attended our Christian club at school and even came to our church youth group. Some got saved!

So now we had been featured in the *RIP* magazine with *Pantera* as the center story, and we were also featured in the top selling rock video that year in our nation!

Yes, I am in a rock video. It is an amazing journey serving God.

*****

In case you may be questioning the truth of this testimony, I have provided a link on YouTube that shows a partial segment of the encounter with Dimebag Darrell.

Pantera vs religious idiots: https://www.youtube.com/watch?v=z7P43M2ZL28.

The following link had contained similar content, but is no longer on *YouTube* because the account has been removed.

Pantera Vs Extreme Christians In A Hotel: https://www.youtube.com/watch?v=yCI85UzOaqk.

19

Where Was I on 9/11?

When you pass through the waters, I will be with you;
and when you pass through the rivers, they will not sweep
over you. When you walk through the fire, you will
not be burned; the flames will not set you ablaze.

—Isaiah 43:2

The Lord is good, a refuge in times of trouble.
He cares for those who trust in Him,

—Nahum 1:7

Be strong and courageous. Do not be afraid or terrified
because of them, for the Lord your God goes with
you; He will never leave you nor forsake you.

—Deuteronomy 31:6

When I am afraid, I put my trust in you.
In God, whose word I praise—
in God I trust and am not afraid.
What can mere mortals do to me?

—Psalm 56:3–4

There are several notable events that people often refer to and ask,
"Where were you when this happened?" One that is often brought

up is "Where were you when President John F. Kennedy was assassinated?"

Most people my age can tell you exactly where they were and what they were doing. I was in the eighth grade, lined up with other students in the hallway, on my way to a pep rally in the school gymnasium.

President Kennedy was assassinated on November 22, 1963, on my husband's sixteenth birthday. My husband was in his tenth-grade history class while history was being made.

Another notable event for people in central Pennsylvania was the meltdown at *Three Mile Island*, the nuclear power plant about 10 miles from where I lived. The Three Mile Island Unit 2 reactor, near Middletown, Pennsylvania, partially melted down on March 28, 1979. This has been listed as the most serious accident in United States commercial nuclear power plant operating history.

I remember that the lady that read the water meter was at our house that morning and ended up staying for over three hours as a "take cover lockdown" was declared for the area. Everyone was told to stay inside a shelter because of the radioactive fallout that had been released. She called into the water company and was told to remain indoors where she was at until she would be cleared to leave later that afternoon.

The woman was not a Christian, but because of the severity of the threat of a possible nuclear meltdown and explosion, she was very willing to listen to everything that I could share with her about Jesus throughout that afternoon! I truly had a captive audience!

I believe most of us can recall where we were, as well as our family members, and what we were doing when the 9/11 attack took place on September 11, 2001. I was, of course, at the school teaching a morning class.

Channel One News was a daily, televised, twelve-minute newscast that was beamed via satellite during the school year to about twelve thousand schools in the Channel One Network community. Their first broadcast was in 1989.

To become part of the Channel One Network community, a school received free color televisions and free wiring and installation in every classroom and office in the school building in exchange for an agreement to broadcast the entire news program every weekday morning to all staff and students to include non-interrupted marketing commercials.

Our school had become part of the *Channel One* Network soon after it emerged; therefore, all classrooms had been furnished with brand new color televisions. Mine was mounted on the wall in the front of my classroom.

It was early in the morning and classes had started for the day. My students were working steadily on their keyboarding assignments. A teacher across the hall from me yelled to me that I should turn on my television because a plane had crashed into one of the towers in New York City. Not realizing what was really happening, I turned on my television in the classroom.

The news channel was playing reruns of the plane crashing into the building, presuming that it had been a navigation error on the part of the pilot. Then, to everyone's horror, a live shot came on showing a second plane crashing into the other tower. The tone of the broadcast drastically changed as it was determined that the crashes were happening on purpose and that the United States was possibly under enemy attack!

The environment of my classroom changed from the normal *got-it-all-under-control* teen atmosphere to visibly shaken, fearful teens who began desperately looking to me for comfort. Their fear increased drastically when the news channel announced that there was a third plane that was currently heading into Pennsylvania. All thoughts went immediately to the possibility that *Three Mile Island* could be the target of the next attack, which would place our school within range of fatality if a nuclear explosion were to happen.

All of my students knew that I was a Christian, but most never pursued personal interest in my faith. However, at that moment in time, realizing that their lives may be in jeopardy, many began asking direct questions about God, His protection, and if Heaven and Hell were real. They particularly wanted to know how to be *saved*.

Even though they were terribly frightened, as I answered many of their questions, I could tell that most of the students began to experience a sense of comfort and safety in my classroom. Because they knew that I was the Advisor to the Christian club and also the Youth Leader at my church, many believed that I had a special connection to God. As Christians, we all do. Foxhole conversions did take place that day!

I truly believe the Holy Spirit was moving in my classroom that morning. I know I was praying constantly, for my students, my family members, their family members, and especially for the people directly suffering from the attacks.

Even after the immediate danger to our area passed when the third plane crashed in southwestern Pennsylvania, students still continued to seek comfort from all the horrifying events of the day. Students from other classes even obtained passes and came to my room for special prayer. News broadcasts became grimmer and grimmer, as first-hand reports were coming from all the locations involved.

It was important for me to maintain my composure and demonstrate my faith and trust in the Lord throughout that day. It was the moment to live my faith and prove my faith to my students, not just talk about it. It goes back to something the Lord had personally revealed to me: *When you can't preach it to teach it, live it to give it.*

20

Pondering

Finally, brethren, whatsoever things are true, whatsoever things
are honest, whatsoever things are just, whatsoever things are pure,
whatsoever things are lovely, whatsoever things are of good report; if
there be any virtue, and if there be any praise, think on these things.
—Philippians 4:8

Great are the works of the Lord; they are
pondered by all who delight in them.
—Psalm 111:2

I will remember the deeds of the Lord; yes, I will
remember your miracles of long ago. I will consider all
your works and meditate on all your mighty deeds.
—Psalm 77:11–12

God has given us the wonderful gift of memory, a gift that enables
us to relive moments in time that were precious to us. I have been
blessed with many fond memories of interactions and relationships
with students during my years of teaching in *Homeroom 109*.

This last chapter is devoted to sharing some special snapshot
moments that go beyond expanded testimonies that have already
been presented in previous chapters. Some of these precious moments

were really humorous and some were sentimental. Each time I ponder them in my heart, I am re-blessed!

I need to emphasize that I really enjoyed my students, especially their teenage humor, as well as many of their playful teenage pranks. I must also confess that I often participated, and sometimes mischievously retaliated, in their shenanigans.

My students knew that I loved them and they knew that I enjoyed them. I know that they could feel the awesome presence of the Holy Spirit in my classroom, and I attribute their respect for me and my every success with them to His presence and His guidance and His intervention.

One of my special sentimental ponderings involves a student whose greatest desire was to graduate, get a good job, and as soon as she could, buy a new car. She had completed my keyboarding course in her tenth-grade year and then worked on the school yearbook staff with me in her senior year. I served as the faculty advisor for the school yearbook that year and worked long hours with the students involved. Several of the students from the editorial staff, including this girl, would often come to my home on weekends to do extra work on the yearbook.

I knew that this girl did not attend a church of her own; however, she once attended a special youth service at our church when our son, Dustin, who was also a student at the school at that time, was speaking. He gave a great salvation message. At the end of his sermon, she was so excited about the Gospel message that she had heard that she exclaimed, "If he takes up an offering, he can have all my money!" It wasn't exactly the normal salvation response, but it was definitely memorable. What is special to me is that I knew that she had really heard that message and I knew that it had touched her heart.

She ultimately graduated, got a great job, and achieved her dream of buying herself a brand-new car. However, on her way to pick up several of her cousins in her new car to go to an event, the car reacted to a faulty drive shaft installation, which disconnected and caused the car to flip. She died in that accident.

I have a wall plaque that was given to me by the students who worked with me on the yearbook staff. Every time I look at the plaque, I am reminded of this girl. The yearbook theme was *Reflections* and the heading on the plaque reads "MEMORIES OF REFLECTIONS ARE YOU MRS. SANDRA L. COOK 1989 WE THANK YOU!" There are ten student names engraved on that plaque, including hers.

Continuing on my pondering journey, two other young ladies also come to mind, and I praise the Lord for His intervention in their lives. Both were loners at the school and both had disabilities that hindered them academically. Both eventually confessed that they felt so lonely and depressed that they had planned to kill themselves in their tenth-grade year. Fortunately, they had been invited to attend one of our church youth group events; they went and they found Jesus.

Both girls became members of the Christian club at the school, both began regularly attending the Manada Gap Church Youth Group, they became best friends, both got saved, and both are still serving the Lord.

The one girl, legally blind, obtained a government job out of high school that she still holds and has advanced admirably through promotions. The other girl married a young man that she met in our church youth group, they have three children, and they are raising their family in the church. What a blessing to read encouraging Godly posts by them on Facebook.

There was a young man attending our school who had recently moved to the United States from Palestine. I could never pronounce his name correctly, so I nicknamed him "Fu-Fu," which he seemed to enjoy.

He was extremely respectful to me. In fact, once, during a class that I was teaching involving developing a database and merging it with the fields created in a Microsoft Word template to create a mail merge, he spoke up to say that he was very upset that such a nice lady was using a word over and over again that in his language had a vulgar meaning. He said that he knew that I did not know what the word meant in his language, but he was having trouble listening to me use the word, especially when he believed that I was a proper woman.

I asked him what word I was using that was so offensive, and he said it was the word *merge*. He explained that in Palestinian, it carried the same meaning as the *f* word in English. And there I was, using it over and over again! I had a tough time completing the instructions for that lesson, as I had to avoid using that word because now the whole class knew what it meant in Palestinian!

I was often assigned outside duty during the lunch periods because the school Principal felt that I carried the respect of the students and that I would handle and enforce school rules. It was not a pleasant duty assignment, as students would try to hide and smoke, and sometimes fights broke out. I always tried to be an example to the students in doing the right thing according to school rules and in being fair and just to all students.

One afternoon, as the lunch period was ending, I spotted Fu-Fu, and he was smoking. As I approached him, he tried unsuccessfully to ditch the cigarette, that turned out to be marijuana. Even though he was always a terrific student in my class and I thought very highly of him, I had to follow the rules and be fair and just. Therefore, I had to turn him in to the school Principal and write up the discipline report on him.

Not only would he face disciplinary action from the school, but using the drug on school property was also a criminal charge that could bring other consequences because of his noncitizen status.

I told him, with tears in my eyes, how much it hurt for me to have to follow through on my duty to report him, and he told me that he understood. He apologized that he had put me in that situation and said that it was his fault for acting so stupid. This actually made me hurt even more.

Fu-Fu did end up getting suspended from school for two weeks. I am not sure what ultimately happened regarding his status with the criminal charge. The most memorable part of the story is that when he returned to school following his suspension, he came to my room and brought me a little stuffed bear as a gift with a note apologizing once again to me. I still have my Fu-Fu bear.

Every Christmas, our family would join together to bless a *Christmas Child*, as we called them. We would usually take them shopping and set an amount that they could spend on gifts for themselves, and sometimes we encouraged them to choose a gift for other family members as well. Occasionally, we would just buy them gifts and deliver them. Often, we would take them to lunch as well.

As we were nearing Christmas break at the school one year, my heart went out to a young man in one of my classes who always appeared so depressed. He was usually dressed in old-looking, tight-fitting clothing that was worn and dirty-looking. I rarely witnessed other students from his class interacting with him. He just seemed sad, poor, and dejected.

I felt like the Lord that year was urging me to make him our *Christmas Child.* In order to make sure that it would be acceptable to buy him gifts at Christmas from our family, I called his home and spoke to his mother, who broke into tears when I explained why I was calling. She told me that the young man's father had passed away and that they were struggling financially. She gave me clothing sizes for him and some specific gift ideas and kept thanking me over and over again for what our family was going to do.

It was the day before Christmas break, and I needed to get out to the store and shop for the young man so that I could give his mother the gifts before school closed that week. Our middle son, Braden, offered to ride along with me to the store to help me select clothing, as he was about the same age as the student.

That evening, after school, it began to snow and freeze on the highways. I had recently purchased a new car that had antilock brakes, that I did not know how to use. I had never driven the new car in the snow. The route to the store involved driving over a mountain that had an L-shaped turn at the very top, just before starting straight down a steep hill on the other side.

Trying to get to the store and have ample time to shop, worried that the stores may close early because of the snow storm, I decided to venture out driving into the midst of the storm. I soon discovered, unfortunately, that travelling in those road conditions was not a wise choice. When I got to the top of the mountain to make the turn, I pressed the brakes to slow down. Instead of slowing down, the car began to slide. It slid around the turn and began sliding, out of control, down the steep hill on the other side of the mountain.

I tried pumping the brakes, but that didn't work. The car slid into the guardrail at least twice on the passenger side of the car where my son was sitting. Each time the car headed to hit the guardrail my son would yell, "Mom, Mom, guardrail!" *Boom!* "Mom, Mom, guardrail!" *Boom!* Then the car spun sideways and began sliding down the hill toward a telephone pole, once again on my son's side of the car. This time he yelled, "MOM, MOM, OH NO, TELEPHONE POLE!" I was praying out loud in the Spirit by this time, and miraculously the car slid up about a foot away from the telephone pole and stopped. I know the power of God stopped that car!

Without getting out to check the damage, I started the car up and pulled slowly back out onto the road. My son asked if we were going to go back home, and I responded that we still needed to get to the store and get the student those clothes.

We pulled into the parking lot of the shopping center, and we then got out to check the damage to the car. The whole passenger side of the car was severely scratched and dented.

We completed our shopping and made it home that evening. I did receive grief from my husband for not coming back home after the wreck, but I followed up the scolding by showing him all the wonderful things our family had purchased for the student!

That evening, we worked together as a family to wrap all the gifts for the young man. The next day, I arranged to meet the student's mother at the school to give her the gifts to place under their tree for Christmas. I asked her not to tell her son where the gifts came from, as I did not want him to feel embarrassed around me. However, she did tell him because he came to me and thanked me following the Christmas break. I was so blessed each time I would see him wearing something that I knew we had given him.

One of my favorite memories was when I had my own son, Dustin, as a student. When I was offered the permanent position at the vocational high school, one of biggest hurdles in making my decision concerned my son.

Dustin had been accepted as a sophomore into the Building Construction and Maintenance Program for that upcoming year, the year I would begin my permanent position as a teacher at the school. Because all students in their tenth-grade year were required to take my course, Dustin realized that I would be one of his teachers and he was very concerned about it. He was worried that others, if they did not like me as a teacher, may transfer their resentment on him or tease him that his mom was a teacher. He indicated that he might have a problem coming to the school if I were teaching there, and that he might change his mind and go to his regular school instead.

Dustin had been in an evangelistic service not long before that where he told us that the Lord had audibly spoken to him to go to the vocational high school and take the construction program because he was being called to build churches and evangelize in them. I did not want to be a block to that calling by accepting the teaching position. I told Dustin that I would not accept the job offer if it caused him to not go to the school. He came up with the compromise that I should accept the job, but I had to promise that I would not reveal to any of the other students that he was my son. I made the promise to him, accepted the position, and he became a student at the school.

It was awkward having Dustin in class, trying to avoid any sign of knowing him. I had to treat him like he was a new student that I had never met. He did not seem to have a problem with treating me like he did not know me, which really did hurt my feelings, I have to admit.

As the weeks went by, Dustin began to realize that the students at the school really liked me as a teacher. He became more relaxed and outgoing in my class, actually helping me out by assisting other students because he had already been introduced at home to much of the curriculum that I was presenting. I required that all three of our children complete a typing program and pass a speed test before they were permitted to work on our computers at home. Dustin was technologically pretty adept.

I kept my promise and did not reveal to Dustin's fellow shop peers that I was his mother. They all had no clue about our relationship. That is, until one day in class when Dustin raised his hand with a question, I called on him, and he addressed me as "Mrs. Mommy" instead of Mrs. Cook. As soon as he said it, he tried to cover it up, but the other guys in his shop immediately picked up on it. Some began to exclaim, "Wait a minute, Mrs. Mommy? You called Mrs. Cook Mrs. Mommy?"

They all began to look back and forth at Dustin, then at me, then back at Dustin, making the comparison that Dustin did look like me—he has the same nose, the blue eyes, and he had the light blond hair. As they continued their investigation, they realized our last names were the same—Dustin Cook and Mrs. Cook. Finally, as they reached their conclusion, they all began to badger Dustin with, "Is that your mother? Is Mrs. Cook your mother?"

Dustin sat at his desk, starring straight down at his keyboard, chuckling. Of course, this was my opportunity, and I looked at him and enunciated very clearly "I...did...not...tell...them!"

As the students left to go back to shop, I could hear them out in the hallway asking Dustin questions about why he never told them I was his mother.

Now, with the word out that I was his mother, Dustin established a whole new relationship with me at the school. This opened the door for him to visit for extra lunch money, to place personal items in my room and in my closet, and to ride with me, and later drive me, to and from school. He definitely took advantage of all the perks of being a teacher's kid.

The following summer, Dustin went on a *Teen Missions* trip to Indonesia where he participated in constructing a church.

As I mentioned earlier, I was often guilty of participating in pranks with my students and was also known to retaliate on their level. I particularly remember one rascally young man who loved to pull pranks on me; I celebrate the victory of the way I got even.

I came into my room from hall duty between classes to begin the session with the group that had just entered my room. As I sat down at my desk to take attendance, I realized that my stapler had been squeezed shut and covered with Scotch tape! Glancing up, I observed the smirk on the culprit who was letting me clearly know that he did it.

Ignoring the prank that had been pulled, I began class and started the students on their assignments. Then, as I often did, I took the sponge from the chalk tray of the blackboard out to the water fountain and soaked it with water. I came back into the room and lightly washed down the blackboard behind my desk and replaced the still soaking-wet sponge back on the chalk tray.

I had my plan. I knew the prankster was working on a project that he would need to print very soon. In order to print, he would have to leave his desk and go to the front corner of the room to retrieve his copy from the printer. I kept track of his progress, and when he was ready to print, I was ready to make my move.

As he went to the printer, away from me, I retrieved the wet sponge. Hiding the sponge behind me, I went to the desk behind his desk and pretended to be observing that student. When he returned to sit down, I quicky and slickly slipped the wet sponge onto his chair and "squish" he sat on it.

I walked back up and sat down at my desk, trying not to laugh as I observed the shock on the student's face. He sat there squirming for a few seconds and then stood up exasperated and proclaimed, "Who put a wet sponge on my chair?"

In a condescending but helpful voice, I calmly replied to him, "It was probably the same culprit that taped up my stapler!"

Then there was the young man who refused to keep on task and work on his typing assignment. It was right before lunch, and he informed me that he was too tired to work. I informed him that if he did not get some work done, I was going to keep him ten minutes after class and make him type while I sang to him. He thought I was kidding.

When the bell rang to go to lunch, I told him that he needed to stay behind. He immediately reminded me that I was required to allow him to eat lunch, and I told him that I would make sure he had time to eat lunch. However, he was going to have to work for ten minutes to make up for the time he did not work during class. If he did not do that, he was going to have to spend his entire lunchtime with me and eat his lunch in my room.

Not wanting to miss the time at lunch with his friends, he started to type. I started playing a song on my CD player, one of my oldies, and began to sing out loud along with the song. He looked at me as though I were crazy. I stopped singing long enough to remind him that I had told him that if he did not work during class, I was going to keep him after class, make him work, and sing to him.

I have occasionally been told that my singing is not very pleasant to listen to. I think I sound okay, but some inform me that I cannot carry a tune. They tell me that I am off-key and sound really bad. My student began audibly verifying this claim. As I continued enthusiastically to belt out the song, he painfully exclaimed, "Mrs. Cook, this is cruel and unusual punishment!"

After that episode, I never had a problem again with that young man not working during my class! In future years I discovered that he grew up and became part of his family's gospel music group!

There was a girl in one of my classes that had been cautioned by administration that if she became involved in one more fight at the school, she would be recommended for permanent expulsion.

She and her brother, who also attended the school, grew up in a tough neighborhood in the city and came from an extremely rough background. Her brother, unfortunately, became deeply involved with drug dealers and was later shot and killed in front of their home.

This young lady was always polite to me in my class, and I was thankful to be able to develop a good relationship with her. She knew that I truly cared about her.

One day at lunch, I was eating at my desk in my classroom, as I often did, trying to get as much work done during the school day as I possibly could so I would have more time with my family in the evenings. As I was about to eat my second chocolate cupcake (there were two in the pack), I heard a commotion starting in the hallway outside my door. I could tell it was leading to a fight as students, girls, began screaming vulgarities at one another.

With my second cupcake in hand, I ran to my classroom door to the hallway, discovering that one of the participants was the girl that would be expelled if she got into one more fight. She and another girl were just about to enter into battle.

Wanting to save her from being expelled, without thinking, I ran to her putting myself between her and the other girl. I put my arm around her neck and shoved the chocolate cupcake into her mouth. She was so shocked dealing with the cupcake in her mouth that I had no trouble pushing her into my room. I shut my door behind us and stood blocking it. She tried to get around me to go back out into the hall, and I commanded her to stop it, explaining to her that I was trying to keep her from getting expelled from the school. I pleaded with her to calm down.

Clearing the cupcake from her mouth, she blurted out, "Mrs. Cook, you are crazy!" Then we hugged each other and began to laugh. She stayed with me in my room until she calmed down, and then I gave her a pass to go back to her class.

Unfortunately, following the death of her brother, she left the school and I did not hear from her again. But I always remember her whenever I see a chocolate *Tastykake* cupcake.

Unable to say "no" when asked to assume more responsibility at the school, especially if it afforded the opportunity to minister, I began teaching some evening classes for a local organization that housed older teenage boys who had been convicted of crimes. Instead of placing these young men in prison, they were incarcerated in group homes.

Part of the rehabilitation program for these young men included educational opportunities, as many of them needed to complete their high school education and graduate. I was asked to teach my Keyboarding and Computer Applications course for them. I taught four quarterly sessions per year.

Every evening before the group arrived, I would walk around the classroom laying my hands on each chair and praying personally for each young man that would be seated at each desk. My heart broke for these boys that were in deep trouble at such a young age.

Normally, the group would work for half the class, take a snack break in the cafeteria, and then return to complete the class. The guards in the classroom were extremely strict and demanded total obedience from each young man. Disobedience to them, or to me, resulted in removal from the class, temporarily or permanently, depending upon the misconduct.

One young man in a keyboarding session was doing an outstanding job and achieving great success in his typing skill. I praised him for his accomplishments, as I was blessed to witness his passion and enthusiasm.

When it became time for the break, I announced to the group to begin to shut their typing program down and prepare to leave. The young man wanted to complete the lesson he was working on, so he tried to keep typing as fast as he could and did not begin to shut down immediately. I waited a couple minutes and then announced again that everyone should shut down and prepare for break. The young man then said out loud that he only had a little to finish and wanted to get it done.

Wow! At that point, to my astonishment and horror, one of the guards went to his desk, shut off his computer, grabbed him by the arm, and lifted him from his chair, shouting in his face, "The lady said 'Stop' and meant 'Stop.' Do you understand?" He then removed the young man from the classroom. He was temporarily suspended from participating in the class.

I truly did not understand the harshness of the reaction of the guard, and the guard could tell I was upset. After removing the young man, he returned to explain to me that the young man was incarcerated because he had been convicted of rape. Part of the rehabilitation was for him to understand and immediately respond to any command from a woman to "stop" whatever needed stopped.

The young man eventually returned to my class and successfully completed the course. Upon his return, he was required to apologize to me. I had a hard time with that.

Many of my students have kept in touch with me following their graduation from the school, particularly the ones that attended our church youth group or those who were involved in the Christian club at the school. To my delight, several couples from those groups ended up getting married. And to my greatest delight, many are now involved in ministry and some have become Pastors! One of my greatest blessings was when I was asked to speak to a youth group that was Pastored by one of my former students.

I do have a sad, unending story of one of my students that has continued for the past twenty years. The young man regularly attended our church youth group, but continuously fought battles with drugs and a bad lifestyle. He would try to convince me, and himself, that he was getting better, but the evidence was never there.

Following his leaving high school, he eventually was imprisoned, and I would regularly receive calls beginning with "You are receiving a call from an inmate from the Dade County Prison." He would always call seeking prayer.

When he was finally released and returned to his home in this area, the Lord impressed me to call him. I was not sure where to call, but I had his home telephone number from where he lived in high school. I called the number and his father answered and gave me his cell phone number.

The young man was totally amazed when I tracked him down. Once again, he was into a bad lifestyle heading for trouble. And as I always did, I prayed with him and tried to counsel him to the Lord.

He eventually moved in with a girl, and they have a son and a daughter. I visited them and took gifts to the children. I continued to pray for him, and often with him, and now also for his family, as he continues to battle the things of this world. I have learned that witnessing and devotion can take a lifetime! His ongoing saga continues, but even more, so does God's grace!

I conclude my pondering by sharing with you my hardest and most emotionally challenging experience in ministry. One of my students, the sister of a regular youth group member, together with her boyfriend, also a student of mine, began to attend the Christian club at the school and eventually the Manada Gap Youth Group as well. The two students were sweethearts all through their school years.

Following graduation, they moved in together and they had a baby who became extremely ill. Several times, I received telephone calls from them and would go to the hospital to pray for their baby. However, one afternoon the telephone call came that the baby had just died. I was asked to come to the hospital as soon as possible if I could.

My husband and I immediately got ready and went to the hospital. When we entered the room where the entire family was gathered together, including grandparents and other close relatives, we encountered a scene that I will never forget. The young mother was lying on a bed, cuddling her baby who was snuggled on her shoulder. The baby appeared to me to be peacefully sleeping, although I knew otherwise.

The young girl immediately got up from the bed and walked over to me, gently carrying her child. Assuredly she told me how she had witnessed angels who entered the hospital room and carried her baby to Heaven. Others in the room agreed that they had seen it as well. What a vision of comfort the Lord had provided for this young grieving mother and her family.

I cannot begin to explain the emotional terror I experienced when the girl handed her baby to me to hold and asked me to lead prayer for her and her family. Although I felt like I was going to faint, I prayed to God for the strength to be strong for the girl and her family. I prayed that the Lord would give me strength to overcome my human fear of holding the deceased child. I prayed that the Lord would give me the right words to share with family members, some who were not saved including the grandparents.

All I can say is that the Lord is faithful to be there when you need Him most. I was able to hold that child lovingly and peacefully as the Holy Spirit brought forth a salvation message that reached the heart of the grandfather, who accepted the Lord that afternoon.

I was able to relate the story of David when his son, born to Bathsheba, died seven days after birth. Although David had fasted and prayed for the healing of the child, the child died. The scripture states that David said that while the child was alive, he fasted and wept. However, when the child died, he realized that he could not bring the child back. The main thing he understood was that even though the child would not return to him, he could go to the child.

Concluding this message in prayer, I challenged the family to be sure that they accept the Lord and are saved because, even though the baby would not return to them during this life, they could, upon their death, go to be reunited with the child in Heaven.

As a prior teacher, I can't seem to go anywhere without running into former students. I am truly blessed when they tell me that I played a special part in touching their lives.

The Lord has impressed to me over the years to write this book. As I have often shared in conversation with others my stories and testimonies of my experiences in *Homeroom 109*, many have urged me to write these down and publish a book.

I pray that sharing my experiences in *Homeroom 109* has touched your heart and blessed you. And I pray that it encourages you to earnestly pray for God's continued anointing on the administrators, teachers, and staff sent as missionaries into our children's schools.

About the Author

Dr. Sandra Jenkins Cook has over thirty years of experience working in education. She began pursuing her college degree after she and her husband, Randy, were married; put it on hold when they became the parents of three dynamic children; and finally completed her Bachelor of Education degree ten years later when her youngest child began kindergarten. She began her teaching career as an Instructor of Secretarial Science at an area community college. She later resigned to follow the Lord's calling to teach at a Christian school where she developed the initial curriculum to add a high school business program. Continuing to pursue God's leading, she went into public education teaching for sixteen years at a vocational high school, where she became the advisor to the first public high school Christian club in the area.

During this same time, she and her husband accepted positions as the Youth Leaders at a rural church. They started with five teenagers at their first service that increased to eighty to one hundred teens attending within the first year. In her latter teaching years, she felt the urging of the Lord to obtain further educational degrees to enter into administrative positions in public education. She received her Master of Education from Penn State University and went on to Temple University to acquire her Secondary Principal Certification and her Vocational Administrative Director Certification. She served in various entry-level administrative positions and ultimately became the Assistant Director of a vocational high school, where she was in charge of all staff and all educational activities and policies at three locations. Obeying the calling of God, she eventually resigned from that position to follow the vision and direction from God to establish a nondenominational, evangelical Christian vocational high school that became the first of its kind in our nation. Her passion is to encourage Christian schools to add Christian vocational programs to their high school offerings. Desiring continued education in Biblical study, Sandra acquired her Doctor of Ministry degree from the Colorado Theological Seminary.